Spotlight on Young Children and ASSESSMENT

Each issue of *Young Children*, NAEYC's award-winning journal, includes a cluster of articles on a topic of special interest and importance to the early childhood community. Most of the selections in this book originally appeared in *Young Children*, vol. 59, no. 1, in the cluster "Child and Program Assessment: Tools for Reflective Educators." Others were written for this book or come from Beyond the Journal (www.naeyc.org), an online collection of resources that complement and expand on articles found in the journal.

Copyright © 2004 by the National Association for the Education of Young Children. All rights reserved. Second printing 2010.

Cover photos: *(front cover, clockwise from top left)* © Jonathan A. Meyers; © Ellen B. Senisi; © Ellen B. Senisi; © Marilyn Nolt; *(middle photo)* © Marilyn Nolt; *(back cover, clockwise from top left)* © Marilyn Nolt; © Joel Goldman; © Paula Jorde Bloom; © Paula Jorde Bloom
Illustrations throughout © Sylvie Wickstrom.

National Association for the Education of Young Children
1313 L Street NW, Suite 500
Washington, DC 20005-4101
202-232-8777 or 800-424-2460

Through its publications program, the National Association for the Education of Young Children (NAEYC) provides a forum for discussion of major issues and ideas in the early childhood field, with the hope of provoking thought and promoting professional growth. The views expressed or implied are not necessarily those of the Association. NAEYC thanks the contributors.

ISBN 978-1-928896-17-3
NAEYC Item #285
Library of Congress Control Number 2004107858
Printed in the United States of America

Contents

2 Introduction/*Derry Koralek*

4 Framing the Assessment Discussion/*Jacqueline Jones*

9 Beyond Outcomes: How Ongoing Assessment Supports Children's Learning and Leads to Meaningful Curriculum/*Diane Trister Dodge, Cate Heroman, Julia Charles, and Jessica Maiorca*

17 Infant/Toddler Assessment: One Program's Experience/*Margo L. Dichtelmiller and Laura Ensler*

22 From Policing to Participation: Overturning the Rules and Creating Amiable Classrooms/*Carol Anne Wien*

29 Research in Review: School Readiness Assessment/*Kelly L. Maxwell and Richard M. Clifford*

38 Ensuring Culturally and Linguistically Appropriate Assessment of Young Children/*Rosa Milagros Santos*

40 Where We Stand on Curriculum, Assessment, and Program Evaluation/*NAEYC and NAECS/SDE*

42 The Words We Use: A Glossary of Terms for Early Childhood Education Standards and Assessment/*Jana Martella*

45 Assessing Children's Development: Strategies That Complement Testing/*Ann S. Epstein, Lawrence J. Schweinhart, and Andrea DeBruin-Parecki*

54 Choosing an Appropriate Assessment System/*Amy Lynn Shillady*

58 Print and Online Resources That Spotlight Young Children and Assessment/*Marian Marion and Gayle Mindes*

61 Reflecting, Discussing, Exploring: Questions and Follow-Up Activities/*Heather Biggar*

Spotlight on Young Children and Assessment

"The check is in the mail."

"This won't hurt a bit."

"Try it, you'll like it."

"Assessment is good for teachers and children."

Only the last of these statements is consistently true. Assessment collects data—information about the progress of individuals or a group of children. When these data are put to use, they can lead to improvements in teaching that allow children to be more effective learners. And assessment data can be shared with families and other stakeholders who want to know whether a curriculum or teaching approach supports desired outcomes for children.

In the expanded version of the recently revised joint position statement, "Early Childhood Curriculum, Assessment, and Program Evaluation: Building an Effective, Accountable System in Programs for Children Birth through Age 8," NAEYC and the National Association of Early Childhood Specialists in State Departments of Education (NAECS/SDE) define assessment as

> A systematic procedure for obtaining information from observation, interviews, portfolios, projects, tests, and other sources that can be used to make judgments about children's characteristics (2003, 27).

This broad definition covers a wide range of appropriate practices in child development programs and schools for children from infancy through the primary years.

What does assessment look like in practice? How is it used? Here are a few examples to show how early childhood educators might carry out their assessment roles.

Illustrations throughout © Sylvie Wickstrom

- Two teachers review and discuss a series of photos of toddlers engaged in various activities. The photos help them think about what went well and what could be improved.

- Teachers notice that a 10-month-old has begun crying inconsolably every morning when her mother leaves. By coordinating their responsibilities, one teacher is able to observe the baby and mother's good-byes so that both teachers will have the information needed to plan ways to help the baby cope with separation.

- A preschool director holds a meeting with families to introduce and describe how the program's screening tools help to identify for further assessment children who may have developmental or health risks. The director invites family members to take part in the screening process.

- Several times a year the kindergartners help their teacher decide which samples of their work they will keep to document what and how they have learned.

- At the end of their project about homes around the world, the second-graders demonstrate their new knowledge by creating individual photo albums, a class bulletin board, and a newsletter for families.

The articles collected in this book address the purposes of and uses for assessment. They give readers an overview of the topic and offer specific examples to show how assessment informs and improves practice in early childhood education.

"Framing the Assessment Discussion," by **Jacqueline Jones,** opens the book with an overview of assessment and the answers to some basic questions about its purpose and focus, appropriate methods, and uses for assessment results.

In "Beyond Outcomes: How Ongoing Assessment Supports Children's Learning and Leads to Meaningful Curriculum," authors **Diane Trister Dodge, Cate Heroman, Julia Charles,** and **Jessica Maiorca** show how educators can use the results of ongoing assessment to plan appropriate ways to respond to children's progress along a continuum of curriculum objectives.

In "Infant/Toddler Assessment: One Program's Experience," **Margo L. Dichtelmiller** and **Laura Ensler** share some important ideas about effective ways to assess infants and toddlers. They describe the experiences of one program as it implements a functional assessment.

In "From Policing to Participation: Overturning the Rules and Creating Amiable Classrooms," **Carol Anne Wien** describes the process by which a group of educators examines and then removes their multiple rules for children's behavior. The teachers' reflections lead to significant changes that transform their practices and children's experiences.

A Research in Review column, "School Readiness Assessment," written by **Kelly L. Maxwell** and **Richard M. Clifford,** and edited by **Diane M. Horm,** uses a question-and-answer format to define and explain what is known about school readiness assessment.

"Ensuring Culturally and Linguistically Appropriate Assessment of Young Children," by **Rosa Milagros Santos,** describes issues related to the assessment of children from diverse backgrounds and summarizes considerations for appropriate assessment.

"Where We Stand on Curriculum, Assessment, and Program Evaluation," by **NAEYC** and **NAECS/SDE,** shares key recommendations for curriculum, assessment, and program evaluation and accountability, as detailed in their 2003 joint position statement.

In "The Words We Use: A Glossary of Terms for Early Childhood Education Standards and Assessment," **Jana Martella** offers definitions of many of the important terms pertaining to assessment of young children.

Ann S. Epstein, Lawrence J. Schweinhart, and **Andrea DeBruin-Parecki,** in "Assessing Children's Development: Strategies That Complement Testing," discuss how authentic assessments such as observations, portfolios, and ratings of children by teachers and parents can provide important information about young children's skills and progress over time. The authors explain the importance of implementing a balanced, child-friendly approach to assessment.

Amy Lynn Shillady provides guidance on the selection of appropriate assessment instruments and a summary of the key characteristics of various assessment systems in "Choosing an Appropriate Assessment System."

— *Derry Koralek*

Framing the Assessment Discussion

Jacqueline Jones

Achieving an understanding of young children's learning is deeply rooted in teachers' powers of observation. Up-close, ongoing observation and recording of what children say and do can yield valuable information about children's interests and emerging understandings. Teachers can use this information to create rich learning environments and to implement effective instructional programs (Chittenden & Courtney 1989; Helm, Beneke, & Steinheimer 1998; Jablon, Dombro, & Dichtelmiller 1999; Jones 2003; Jones & Courtney 2003). However, across the pre-K-to-12 continuum, the national focus on professional accountability and quality programming has evolved into a call for more and more testing of younger and younger children (Barton 1999).

It is reasonable to ask for evidence of how young children are developing and learning. It is also reasonable to ask if early childhood programs are providing the most appropriate and effective learning environments. As portfolios of children's work compete with percentile scores, the nature of the evidence used to answer questions about children's progress and program quality has become a matter of considerable debate and angst.

In the current climate, responsible early childhood educators need to reach beyond enhancing their skills in observation and documentation to developing what Stiggins (1991) calls *assessment literacy*—a deep understanding of the uses and limitations of the full range of assessment options, the knowledge to select the most appropriate methods to describe the development of young children. These options may include teachers' anecdotal notes, samples of children's drawings and constructions, and records of their conversations, as well as a variety of assessment results from more formal instruments.

Photos © BmPorter/Don Franklin

As the accountability/testing debate continues, young children need assessment-literate advocates who are equipped not only with enhanced powers of observation and documentation but also with the knowledge and skills to participate in an assessment-related discourse that is grounded in the basic principles of sound assessment practice.

Jacqueline Jones, PhD, is the director of early childhood initiatives at Educational Testing Service in Princeton, New Jersey. She studies the development of effective early childhood assessment systems and assessment-related professional development for early childhood educators.

Assessment and testing

For some time we have known that accurate assessment of young children's learning is a complicated process (Dyer 1973; Shepard 1994; Shepard, Kagan, & Wurtz 1998). The rapid and episodic learning that is a hallmark of early childhood is a significant assessment challenge. Young children may or may not fully engage in a structured assessment task, and their understandings may look very different from week to week. Although the number of screening, diagnostic, and achievement instruments has increased over the years, there is little doubt that most standardized measures provide a very limited view of early learning.

As the tension between quality instruction and testing increases, a fundamental distinction needs to be made between testing and the process of assessment. Assessment may be defined as the ongoing process of gathering evidence of learning in order to make informed judgments about instructional practice. This process occurs continually in almost every early childhood classroom as teachers listen to children's conversations, observe their actions, and make judgments about the progress of an individual child or a group of children.

A test has been defined as "a systematic procedure for eliciting and measuring comparable samples of behavior" (ETS 2003, 27). Tests usually provide a quick look at specific behaviors at a particular point in time. They produce just one type of evidence that might be gathered in the overall assessment process.

Appropriate assessment is an integral part of the teaching/learning process, and sound assessment practices can

- highlight children's knowledge, skills, and interests;
- document their growth over time;
- describe children's progress toward specified learning goals; and
- provide constructive feedback to instructional programs.

> **By** providing a record of children's growth over time, assessment can become **an advocate for children and the centerpiece for meaningful conversations between families and educators.**

Done well, the assessment process can be a powerful tool for teachers. By providing a record of children's growth over time, assessment can become an advocate for children and the centerpiece for meaningful conversations between families and educators.

Framing the assessment discourse

Discussions focused on accountability and testing need to be framed around a few fundamental and critical assessment-related issues. The following questions do not represent an exhaustive set of the major issues in accountability and the testing of young children. Rather, they attempt to suggest some basic interrelated assessment concerns that teachers, administrators, and parents who use assessment information should pose and be able to challenge if they wish to participate in the accountability debate.

What is the purpose of the assessment?

Shepard, Kagan, and Wurtz (1998) outline four major purposes of early childhood assessment:

- the support of learning,
- identification of special needs,
- program evaluation and monitoring of trends, and
- high-stakes accountability.

Although the primary purpose of early childhood assessment is to improve instruction, identifying special needs and monitoring program quality are also legitimate needs.

A teacher who needs to gather information about particular children's progress in developing science concepts might collect the children's drawings, take photographs of their constructions, and make records of their conversations. Classroom- and curriculum-based assessments can help teachers plan more appropriate instructional practices because these assessments are directly tied to instruction and allow a close look at individual children. However, an administrator may need to collect evidence to understand if an instructional program has been effective and how children seem to be progressing toward a set of learning goals. In this case, it may be helpful to have a sample group of children perform a comparable task that reflects the desired learning goals.

When information about individual children is not needed, evidence about the quality of the educational program might come from assessing a sample of children rather than an entire population. The results, or scores, from such a task are one part of the evidence that the administrator can use to evaluate program effectiveness and to monitor children's progress.

Clarifying the purpose of the assessment is a preliminary step in decision making about

- the content and type of knowledge to be assessed;
- the population to be assessed (for example, a subset of children or an entire population);
- the most appropriate assessment method and instrument;
- the target audience for the assessment information—teachers, parents, policy makers, the children themselves; and
- the formats in which assessment results will be reported to the target audience.

What content and type of knowledge is being assessed?

The content and type of knowledge to be assessed is critical in determining the assessment method and instrument. Stiggins (2000, 2001) proposes moving beyond simply identifying a curriculum domain such as reading or science to aligning assessment methods with the most appropriate assessment targets.

Assessment targets or types of knowledge to be assessed consist of

Knowledge mastery—Does Mary know her address? Can Steven spell his name?

Patterns of reasoning—How does Helen go about recording her observations of the class gerbil?

Performance skill—Can John pour his milk into a glass without spilling it?

Product development capabilities—Can Susan build a cardboard model of her house?

Dispositions—Does Sam really enjoy listening to stories and pretending to read?

What is the most appropriate assessment method?

Defining the assessment purpose and the content and type of knowledge to be assessed forms the groundwork for selection of the most suitable assessment method and instrument. Evidence of a child's ability to perform a specified task may or may not reveal her attitudes and dispositions. For example, reading fluently and with comprehension does not, by itself, reveal a love of literature.

> **E**arly childhood educators need to understand the **range of appropriate assessment options, from classroom-based to norm-referenced measures.**

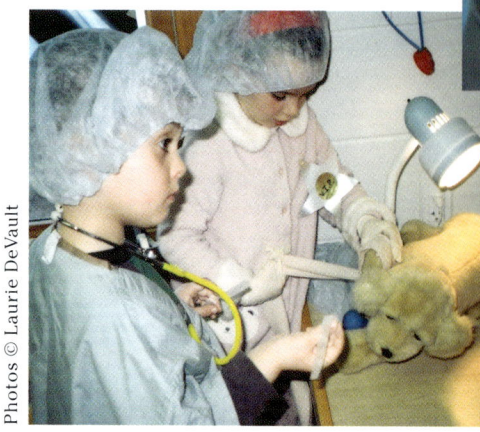
Photos © Laurie DeVault

While evidence of reading performance may be gathered by engaging a child in an actual reading task, further exploration, through observation or interview, might be needed to understand the child's attitudes about books.

Early childhood educators need to understand the range of appropriate assessment options, from classroom-based to norm-referenced measures. Sound early childhood assessment systems incorporate multiple assessment methods to meet a variety of needs (Jones 2003).

How will the assessment results be evaluated?

Samples of children's work, teachers' anecdotal notes, and performances on standardized measures are eventually evaluated against appropriate learning goals and standards, the performance of a similar group of children, or a scoring rubric. At some point an informed judgment or evaluation must be made that will modify an instructional program, generate further assessment, or provide feedback on program quality.

> Mrs. Kay knows that by the end of fourth grade her current first-graders are expected to have mastered a New Jersey Habits of Mind science standard: *Keep records that describe observations, carefully distinguish actual observations from ideas and speculation, and are understandable weeks and months later.* She has designed a unit around the topic of silkworms in which the children conduct regular ongoing observa-

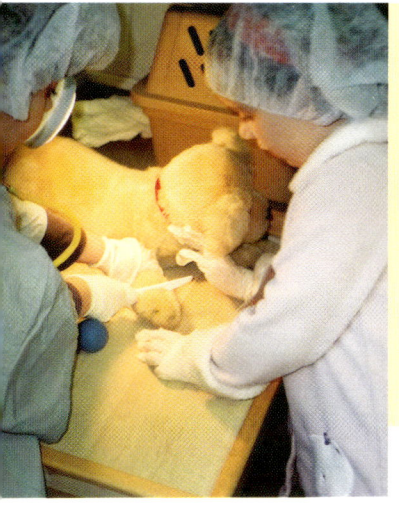

tions of developing silkworms, engage in group discussions about their observations, and keep science journals in which they draw and write their observations and impressions. All classroom-based and formal assessment information is weighed against the children's progress toward the science standard.

Carefully gathered evidence is of little use unless it begins to answer questions about how young children are developing and learning and if programs are providing the most appropriate and effective learning environments. Therefore, the learning goals and standards must be appropriate, and any comparison groups must be as similar as possible to the child or group being assessed.

Are assessment results reported clearly and accurately?

Understanding assessment results can be daunting. The most well-constructed and appropriate assessment is useless if the target audience cannot understand the results. Assessment developers are responsible for ensuring that assessment results are clear and accurate, and consumers of assessment information are responsible for engaging in the assessment process with as much assessment-related knowledge and expertise as possible (Popham 2000, 2002). Young children and educators are not well served when instructional and policy decisions are made on the basis of assessment results that the target audience does not understand.

How are the assessment results to be used?

Perhaps the most important element of any assessment is the ultimate use of the assessment information (Messick 1992). Decisions to extend a lesson for a few additional days, to identify a child as needing special services, or to provide additional resources to a program constitute uses of assessment data that should be linked to the stated purpose of the assessment process, aligned to intended use of the assessment method or instrument, and based on a thorough understanding of the assessment results. According to Standard 1.1 in *Standards for Educational and Psychological Testing,* "A rationale should be presented for each recommended interpretation and use of test scores, together with a comprehensive summary of the evidence and theory bearing on the intended use of interpretation" (AERA, APA, & NCME 1999, 17). The ultimate use of any assessment data should be aligned with the stated purpose of the assessment and should cause no harm.

Photos © Ellen B. Senisi

The ultimate use of any assessment data should be **aligned with the stated purpose** of the assessment and should **cause no harm.**

ASSESSMENT   **7**

Conclusion

Snow and Jones (2001, 60) argue that "tests, by themselves, cannot improve educational outcomes. They can lead to improvement only if they become a stimulus to change in the educational system—a basis for improved curricula, upgraded instruction, better professional development for teachers, and better distribution of resources."

The assessment issues described here are basic to a reasoned discourse on accountability and testing of young children. If the conversation is based on principles of sound measurement practice, the fields of early childhood education and educational measurement will be challenged in new ways to act as responsible advocates for children.

Early childhood teacher preparation programs have the opportunity and the challenge to enhance their assessment-related content so that candidates have a repertoire of assessment strategies and the knowledge and skills needed for accurate use and interpretation of assessment data. In addition, programs can model a range of sound assessment practices as they monitor the progress of candidates in preparation programs (Stiggins 1999; Hyson 2003).

Educators can become better advocates for young children when they begin to demystify assessment and testing and come to understand the strengths and limitations of the range of assessment options. As educators build their assessment literacy, they can inform families and hold legislators responsible for supporting sound assessment practices for young children and the programs that serve them.

References

AERA, APA, & NCME (American Educational Research Association, American Psychological Association, & the National Council on Measurement in Education). 1999. *Standards for educational and psychological testing.* Washington, DC: American Educational Research Association.

Barton, P.E. 1999. *Too much testing of the wrong kind; too little of the right kind in K–12 education.* Princeton, NJ: Policy Information Center, Educational Testing Service.

Chittenden, E., & R. Courtney. 1989. Assessment of young children's reading: Documentation as an alternative to testing. In *Emerging literacy: Young children learn to read and write,* eds. D.S. Strickland & L.M. Morrow, 107–20. Newark, DE: International Reading Association.

Dyer, H.S. 1973. Testing little children: Some old problems in new settings. *Childhood Education* 49 (7): 362–67.

ETS (Educational Testing Service). 2003. *Understanding standard-based assessment: Program summary.* Pathwise series. Princeton, NJ: Author.

Helm, J.H., S. Beneke, & K. Steinheimer. 1998. *Windows on learning: Documenting young children's work.* New York: Teachers College Press.

Hyson, M., ed. 2003. *Preparing early childhood professionals: NAEYC's standards for programs.* Washington, DC: NAEYC.

Jablon, J.R., A.L. Dombro, & M. Dichtelmiller. 1999. *The power of observation.* Washington, DC: Teaching Strategies.

Jones, J. 2003. *Early literacy assessment systems: Essential elements.* Princeton, NJ: Policy Information Center, Educational Testing Service.

Jones, J., & R. Courtney. 2003. Documenting early science learning. In *Spotlight on young children and science,* eds. D. Koralek & L.J. Colker, 27–32. Washington, DC: NAEYC.

Messick, S. 1992. *The interplay of evidence and consequences in the validation of performance assessments.* Princeton, NJ: Educational Testing Service.

Popham, J.W. 2000. *Testing! Testing! What every parent should know about school tests.* Needham Heights, MA: Allyn & Bacon.

Popham, J.W. 2002. Ten "must-know" facts about educational testing. *Our Children* 28 (3): 4–6.

Shepard, L.A. 1994. The challenges of assessing young children appropriately. *Phi Delta Kappan* 75 (6): 206–12.

Shepard, L., S.L. Kagan, & E. Wurtz, eds. 1998. *Principles and recommendations for early childhood assessments.* Washington, DC: National Education Goals Panel.

Snow, C.E., & J. Jones. 2001. Making a silk purse: How a national system of annual testing might work. *Education Week,* 25 April, 60.

Stiggins, R.J. 1991. Assessment literacy. *Phi Delta Kappan* 72 (7): 534–39.

Stiggins, R.J. 1999. Evaluating classroom assessment training in teacher education programs. *Educational Measurement: Issues and Practice* 18 (1): 23–27.

Stiggins, R.J. 2000. *Specifications for a performance-based assessment system for teacher preparation.* Portland, OR: National Council for Accreditation of Teacher Education.

Stiggins, R.J. 2001. *Student-involved classroom assessment.* Upper Saddle River, NJ: Prentice Hall.

Beyond Outcomes

How Ongoing Assessment Supports Children's Learning and Leads to Meaningful Curriculum

Diane Trister Dodge, Cate Heroman, Julia Charles, and Jessica Maiorca

Diane Trister Dodge, MS, is the founder and president of Teaching Strategies, Inc., in Washington, D.C., and the lead author of numerous publications, including *The Creative Curriculum,* Child Development Associate training materials, and parent resources. She has 40 years of experience as a teacher, trainer, and curriculum developer.

Cate Heroman, MEd, is director of preschool initiatives for Teaching Strategies, Inc. Cate is a coauthor of *The Creative Curriculum for Preschool* and *The Creative Curriculum Developmental Continuum.*

Julia Charles, MA, is an early childhood special education teacher with the Los Angeles Unified School District at El Sereno Early Education Center. Julia focuses on aligning curricular goals based on assessment to support children's learning in a diverse, inclusive preschool setting.

Jessica Maiorca, MA, is an early childhood special education teacher with the Los Angeles Unified School District at Murchison Early Education Center. Jessica uses assessment to help provide developmentally appropriate curricular experiences for preschool children in an inclusive classroom.

As the public becomes increasingly aware of the potential of early childhood programs to prepare children, especially vulnerable children, for success in school, the pressures on programs to produce positive results have grown. Legislators, boards of education, and funding organizations want to be sure that their investments in early childhood programs are paying off and that children are attaining the standards. For Head Start programs Congress has mandated specific outcomes for preschool children, and standardized tests are being used to determine whether individual programs are achieving the desired results.

At a time when we know so much more about the role of a comprehensive curriculum and ongoing assessment linked to curriculum planning, the danger is that the mandates for outcomes can lead us off in the wrong direction. We must guard against using assessment simply to satisfy mandates and keep in mind how ongoing assessment supports children's learning and leads to meaningful curriculum.

Ongoing assessment is the process of gathering information in the context of everyday class activities to obtain a representative picture of children's abilities and progress. Researchers recommend assessing children based on observations of the processes children use rather than on simple, concrete, disconnected indicators or milestones (Cicchetti & Wagner 1990; McCune et al. 1990; Hauser-Crane & Shonkoff 1995). Data should be collected in a variety of ways: observing and documenting what children do and say;

collecting samples of children's work over time; talking with children to learn more about their thinking; exchanging information with families. The data teachers collect from ongoing assessment enable them to learn more about each child, plan for children's learning, track children's progress, and, when required, generate outcomes reports. Research has shown that when teachers use a comprehensive curriculum and assessment system effectively, children are well prepared for school and do well academically and socially (Campbell et al. 2002; HHS 2003).

The problem is that assessment information is of limited value unless teachers understand what it means and know how to use it to guide children's learning. Too often assessment results are seen as an end product rather than as knowledge that opens the door to learning about each child and to planning meaningful curriculum. Ongoing, classroom-based assessment enables teachers to answer important questions:

• What are children doing and thinking?
• What should I assess?
• What did I learn?
• How should I use what I learned to plan the curriculum?

In this article we describe how ongoing assessment can be a manageable and dynamic process directly linked to planning curriculum and supporting each child's learning and development.

What are children doing and thinking? The role of a curriculum

Before teachers can begin to use a systematic approach to assessment, they need to be confident about what is happening in their classrooms. This is where a comprehensive curriculum comes in; it provides the road map for putting the program in place. A comprehensive curriculum grounded in research and child development theory provides a framework for what to teach, how to teach, and how to assess children's learning. Early childhood educators have a responsibility to "implement curriculum that is thoughtfully planned, challenging, engaging, developmentally appropriate, culturally and linguistically responsive, comprehensive, and likely to promote positive outcomes for all young children" (NAEYC & NAECS/SDE 2003, 1).

Teachers should be knowledgeable about their curriculum and know how to build a comfortable and engaging learning environment for a group of children. This means, at a minimum,

• getting to know children and families
• setting up a classroom with clearly defined interest areas and well-organized and labeled materials that invite children to explore and discover

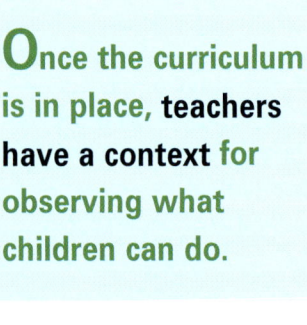

Once the curriculum is in place, teachers have a context for observing what children can do.

Photos © Elisabeth Nichols

- establishing a structure for each day, including a daily schedule and routines, so children know what is expected and experience a sense of order
- helping children learn how to function in a group, relate positively to others, and solve problems peacefully
- helping children build content knowledge and develop the skills and attitudes necessary to be successful learners

Once the curriculum is in place, teachers have a context for observing what children can do as they work in interest areas, participate in large- and small-group activities, and go through the routines of the day. These observations, collected over time, become the basis for decision making. They are the building blocks of assessment. Let's look at an example.

Four-year-olds Maria, Danielle, and Jacob are in the dramatic play area pretending to be at a restaurant. Their teacher writes down the following exchange:

Maria: Can I take your order?

Danielle: Sure, I want spsghetti and meatballs.

Jacob: That's not how you say it! It's spuh-get-e.

Danielle: Spuh-get-e.

Maria: I know what she's saying. Let me write it down. [Maria writes SPGTE and METBLS. Jacob scribbles.] Is that all?

Danielle: Oh, yeah . . . I want some tea too. [Maria writes T. Jacob makes more scribbles.]

Jacob: I'll start cooking and you set the table. [Jacob puts white yarn and red pom-poms in a pot and stirs.]

Documenting what you see and hear enables you to reflect on what you learned about the children and gain valuable insights about each child. The key is to observe purposefully and document examples that provide rich data. This means becoming very familiar with the curriculum's goals and objectives and keeping them in mind when observing children and planning.

What should I assess? Keeping goals and objectives in mind

There are so many different observations teachers could document. How do teachers know which ones will reveal something important about a child? In deciding what to assess, consider these questions:

- What are the goals and objectives of the curriculum I am implementing?
- Which outcomes am I required to gather information about?
- What are the children like individually and as a group?
- Are there specific concerns that need my attention?

> **Goals and objectives** are where you want to take children.
> **Curriculum** is the road map for getting there.
> **Assessment** is a way of ensuring that children are making progress.
> **A continuum for each objective** shows all the steps along the way.

In a comprehensive curriculum, goals and objectives address all aspects of development: cognitive, socio-emotional, language, and physical (NAEYC & NAECS/SDE 2003). Within each developmental area there are broad goals for children's learning.

Cognitive development: children's thinking skills, including the development of logical and symbolic thinking, problem-solving skills, and approaches to learning.

Language development: children's ability to communicate through words, both spoken and written, including listening and speaking, reading and writing skills.

Social/emotional development: children's feelings about themselves, the development of responsibility, and their ability to relate positively to others.

Physical development: children's gross and fine motor skills.

These goals are based on knowledge of child development and widely recognized expectations for preschool children. Goals can be broken down into appropriate objectives. Children learn so much when engaged in meaningful, engaging experiences that it is not practical for teachers to formally assess each and every skill or concept a child has learned. As a result, curriculum developers often struggle with how specific goals and objectives should be. When the goals and objectives are clear and concise yet broad enough to allow children to attain them in many different ways, positive child outcomes can result.

Goals and objectives should also reflect content standards for different disciplines—literacy, math, science, social studies, the arts, and technology—and

Reflection	Related Curriculum Objectives
All the children played cooperatively in the dramatic play area.	Plays well with other children
The children had background knowledge about restaurants and food and applied it to their play.	Applies knowledge or experience to a new context
They used appropriate vocabulary words and expanded sentences in their play.	Expresses self using words and expanded sentences
They seemed to understand the rules of a conversation.	Actively participates in a conversation
Danielle and Jacob were paying attention to the separate syllables in spoken words.	Hears and discriminates the sounds of language
Jacob made scribbles to represent words.	Writes letters and words
Maria used her knowledge of letter sounds to write words.	Uses tools for writing and drawing
Jacob used yarn and pompoms to represent spaghetti and meatballs.	Takes on pretend roles and situations
	Makes believe with objects

address the outcomes requirements and state expectations. Most states have developed, or are in the process of developing, early learning standards for children under five, and the Head Start Outcomes Framework (Head Start Bureau 2001) addresses content standards. A broadly stated objective, such as "Compares and measures," can accommodate more specific federal or state requirements, such as "Identifies longer/shorter." Supporting documentation can demonstrate that a child has an understanding of this concept. Thus, teachers can be confident they are heading in the right direction when implementing a curriculum with broadly stated goals and objectives.

Just as we stay focused on the destination when we use a road map to plan our route, teachers need to keep the curriculum's objectives in mind throughout the day. Prominently displaying the goals and objectives reminds teachers and classroom visitors of the value of the activities children are engaged in at any time of the day. They can observe what children are doing and reflect on specific objectives being addressed.

A brief, factual observation such as the one provided earlier (previous page) offers a great deal of information about the three children, when viewed from the perspective of the curriculum's goals and objectives (see chart, above). Thus this short dramatic play episode serves as a good starting point for assessing what these children already know and can do. Documented observations are among the many pieces of evidence that will lead you to make informed decisions about a child's progress. The more documentation you collect—written observations, writing and art samples, photographs, audio and video recordings—the stronger and more valid your decisions will be.

What did I learn? The value of viewing objectives on a continuum

After you have determined a child's progress in relation to an objective, you can make decisions about appropriate next steps. However, children don't accomplish an objective all at once. They typically go through a series of levels that teachers can anticipate. Knowing this developmental sequence and using it to plan for children with a range of abilities opens the door to truly getting to know each child and being able to structure opportunities for learning.

When an assessment system is based on the curriculum objectives and shows a developmental continuum, teachers can more easily pinpoint what a child knows and is able to do. A continuum describes the phases children experience as they move toward accomplishing a given objective. It provides a way of looking at what children can do and how teachers can plan for the next step. Many assessment systems, such as the Creative Curriculum developmental continuum assessment system for ages 3–5 (Dodge, Colker, & Heroman 2001), identify a typical developmental sequence for the stated objectives. In addition, math experts have defined "learning paths" for children ages three to six (NAEYC & NCTM 2002), and literacy specialists describe a continuum for children's development in early reading and writing (IRA & NAEYC 1998). These various continuums allow for the fact that development is uneven, that all children will not be at the same level at the same time

> **A continuum describes the phases children experience as they move toward accomplishing a given objective.**

in all aspects of development, and that children of the same age will exhibit a range of skills that are typical.

As an example, let's use the objective we identified for Maria, Danielle, and Jacob: "Writes letters and words." A continuum might show a sequence of steps for this objective. Based on the sample observation, the teacher can make some preliminary judgments about Maria's and Jacob's progress along the continuum for the curriculum objective "Writes letters and words" (below). Jacob, who uses scribble writing, appears to be at Step 1. Maria, who wrote SPGTE for spaghetti, appears to be at Step 3, "Uses letters that represent sounds in writing words." Both children are engaged in the same play episode, but they are at entirely different stages of development for this objective. Of course, before making a final determination of the skill level, the teacher will collect more evidence related to this objective.

While these steps show a continuum of development for children ages three to five, there are many behaviors that lead up to Step 1 and many steps that follow Step 3. To make assessment more inclusive of those who are not yet at the Step 1 phase, it is helpful to think about the emerging behaviors, sometimes referred to as *precursors* or *forerunners,* that come before Step 1. For the objective "Writes letters and words," some examples of emerging behaviors include

- scribbles with crayons
- experiments with writing tools such as markers and pencils

Children who remain at this stage of development for a given objective may have a developmental delay or may simply lack experience or opportunity, such as using paper and writing tools at home.

In addition, some children may be at the other end of the spectrum and exceed the widely held expectations

> **T**he essence of developmentally appropriate practice is knowing **where children are on a continuum of learning** and then offering them challenging yet achievable experiences to **gently nudge them along the way.**

for most children ages three to five. All teachers want children to progress, no matter what phase of development they are in; there's always a next step. The essence of developmentally appropriate practice is knowing where children are on a continuum of learning and then offering them challenging yet achievable experiences to gently nudge them along the way.

Teachers keep track of a child's progress for a variety of reasons: to be assured that learning and development are taking place, to make children's progress visible to parents, and to make adjustments in their teaching strategies. Keeping track of children's progress in a systematic way also allows you to look at the status of the entire class and how a group of children is progressing.

Once you have mapped a child's or group of children's development on a continuum, you have completed a major step in the assessment process. Now it is time to use what you have learned to inform your teaching.

How should I use what I learned? Planning for each child and the group

The everyday decisions you make—about the activities and experiences you plan, the content you address, the context in which the learning takes place, the changes you make in the environment—are based on your knowledge of each child and of the group as a whole. Deciding how to use your assessment information in the classroom may seem like an overwhelming task. It would be nice to have a handy set of directions or a prescription that would tell you exactly what to do next to achieve a desired result. However, children are not robots we can program for a predictable response. You have to consider many factors, such as a

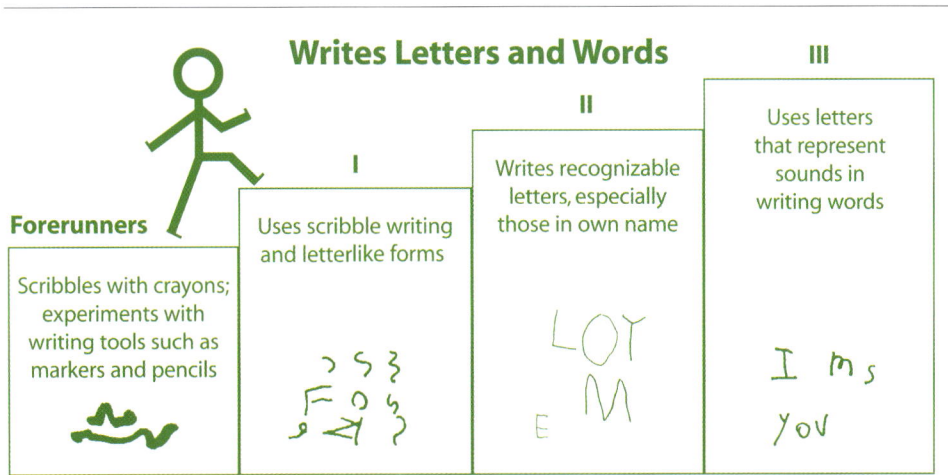

From The Creative Curriculum Developmental Continuum for Ages 3–5. Reproduced by permission from D.T. Dodge, L.S. Colker, and C. Heroman, *The Creative Curriculum Developmental Toolkit for Ages 3–5* (Washington, DC: Teaching Strategies, 2001), 17.

At our weekly team meeting, we talked about how the children needed more experiences in writing letters and words. We checked to be sure we had plenty of writing materials not only in the library area but throughout the classroom: paper, crayons, markers, and large pencils; magnet letters, letter stamps, and cards with each child's name. Looking at the continuum for this objective made us realize that a few children would be scribbling with crayons and drawing simple pictures; some would make scribbles that contained letterlike forms; some would write recognizable letters, especially those in their own name; and a few children would be using letters that represent sounds in words. Knowing the sequence for this objective made us more aware of what to look for as children write and draw during their play.

We can also anticipate what the next step is for every child, so we can help each child make progress. For example, if we notice a child who is beginning to make letterlike forms in his scribbling, we could see if he is aware of this. If not, we could point it out: "Look, Tyrone, you made a mark that looks like a *T*, just like the first letter in your name. Can you make another one like it?" In this way we can encourage a child to become more purposeful about what he is doing. We now have a clearer idea of our role.

Photos by Casey Sills

child's culture, language, strengths, interests, temperament, and learning style.

It is reassuring to discover that, having used the goals and objectives regularly in observing children and in weekly planning, you are already involved in the assessment process. In planning for each child, keep assessment information handy so you can refer to it frequently. This will remind you of children's strengths and help you anticipate what different children are likely to do with the materials and activities you provide. With this information in mind, you can observe children during their play and respond appropriately.

For example, the teacher knows that Jacob uses scribble writing and letterlike forms. She then reflects on how she can extend Jacob's learning. What will she do and say that will support him as he moves along the continuum? When Jacob works in other areas of the classroom, she can intentionally offer him writing materials to use in his play: "Jacob, would you like to make an Open sign for your block building?" Or when Jacob wants a turn at the easel, she can ask him to write his name on the sign-up sheet.

The planning process is much more manageable when teaching teams—all those working with a child or group of children—meet together. They can discuss children individually and decide what some logical next steps might be for the child. In addition, a teaching team can review class profiles or summary sheets and make informed decisions about what should happen for the group as a whole. Having used the objectives to decide what materials to display and to plan small- and large-group activities, teachers can now prepare for children with a range of abilities by keeping in mind the different expectations for each level. See the description on page 14 for an example of how this happens.

By planning with developmental steps in mind, teaching teams are more aware of how to guide children's learning and ultimately accomplish curriculum goals. They can anticipate the needs of children and create as well as adapt materials for a broad range of abilities, to better scaffold learning.

Using assessment to reach every child and family

The most powerful outcome of ongoing assessment is the positive relationships teachers can build with each child. Every child is different, but the one thing every child needs is to feel accepted and appreciated. Some children are easy to get to know and like. They readily draw adults into a positive relationship. Others are more challenging, making it hard for adults to see their positive attributes and build positive relationships. These are the children who need us the most (Dodge, Colker, & Heroman 2002). Research shows that the quality of children's relationships with their preschool teachers is an important predictor of children's future social relationships and academic success in school (Peisner-Feinberg et al. 2000). The systematic approach to observing children opens the door to appreciating each child's unique qualities and strengths. This gives teachers a way to build a positive relationship.

A system of ongoing assessment also helps teachers build a relationship with each child's family. Families are already teachers' partners in caring for and educating their children. They are an invaluable source of information about their children's unique life experiences, special interests and needs, and learning styles. In turn, families want to find out what their children's teachers know about their children and what progress they are making.

> **The planning process is much more manageable when teaching teams meet together.**

Most family members don't have a background in child development, and many are unsure about typical expectations for their child's age group. The assessment process provides a wealth of very specific information that teachers can share with families. When family members see how much teachers know about their child and the ways they are supporting their child's development and learning, they gain a greater appreciation for what is happening in the program. In discussing a particular area of development with a family, you can show them the continuum for specific objectives to provide a realistic picture of how children grow and what they might be expected to learn next.

A continuum is important at IEP (Individualized Education Program) meetings where goals and objectives must be written with realistic expectations that a child can meet. Including families in this process builds a true partnership. Family members feel that they have participated in a meaningful way to plan for their child's continued progress. They are also more likely to support their child's learning as they work on the same goals and objectives at home. One preschool teacher at an urban school shares how she partners with families, using a continuum as a resource:

> Jamie is a four-and-a-half-year-old child whose family has experienced many changes in housing, jobs, child care, and family structure. Jamie has a very difficult time separating from family members, handling transitions at school, and making friends. She has frequent tantrums and extended periods of crying. To understand Jamie's behavior and what that might be saying to us, we looked at the developmental continuum. In the areas of physical, language, and cognitive development, Jamie displayed rather typical progress. However, in the area of social/emotional development, Jamie demonstrates many skills in the forerunner stage. This revealed to us that the expectations we held for her were unrealistic. With this new information we could plan ways in which to move Jamie step-by-step along the continuum.
>
> One of Jamie's strengths revealed through the assessment process is her ability to create detailed representational drawings and combine colors creatively. Capitalizing on this ability, we will structure activities that invite other children to join Jamie in art experiences. We will use Jamie as the expert, encouraging her to share how she drew her flowers with the other children. We will implement use of visual cues, such as using our picture schedule to ease her through transitions. We will make drawings showing facial emotions and use them as cues to help her identify and label feelings. We will also set up situations through role-playing, observation, and literature to help Jamie build friendships.
>
> To involve Jamie's mother in our planning and to gather more information, we invited her to a conference. Knowing that parents can be sensitive, we began by talking about Jamie's strengths. In discussing the social/emotional objectives, we used the continuum to explain each step and then asked Jamie's mom where *she* saw Jamie. Although there were some discrepancies in where we placed her development on the continuum, for the most part we concurred. We then shared our plans for Jamie in the classroom. Together, we developed a plan of intervention strategies to use at home, and we scheduled a follow-up meeting.

Reporting to others—A last step

As a very last step in the assessment process, the information teachers have gathered and used to plan curriculum and to support each child's learning can be used to report on group progress. As advocates for developmentally appropriate practice, it is important for early childhood professionals to share what children are learning with those outside their programs. This information may be shared with many stakeholders: administrators, government officials, funding organizations, families, and the general public.

A program that is required to report children's progress on specific indicators—as in Head Start or in some states—needs to have a way to connect children's assessment data with these indicators. While this can be done by hand, it can be very tedious and time-consuming. Many comprehensive assessment systems have electronic solutions—either software or online services—to make the task easier. For example, the Creative Curriculum planning and assessment system enables teachers to create electronic portfolios, complete with samples of children's work. A child's progress is then marked on the continuum online. This Internet-based technology offers appropriate activities and strategies to help a child progress to the next step.

A class profile quickly shows teachers the names of children who are at each step on the continuum for each objective. This makes planning for small groups of children more in tune with the needs of the children. Families can share observations of their children online with teachers. Narrative reports summarizing children's progress are simplified using online assessment systems. Online curriculum planning and assessment systems help teachers streamline their work so they can spend more time with children. And the data from assessment generates outcomes reports automatically.

Conclusion

We have described a way to make assessment a natural process of observing what children can do and of planning curriculum to support their learning. Teachers use curriculum objectives to focus their observations of what children can do. Having gathered purposeful observations, teachers can reflect on what they learned and use the data to plan for each child and the group. When assessment is seen as a meaningful and dynamic part of working with young children, and when it is linked to the curriculum, teachers gain the true benefits of ongoing assessment. They are also likely to find teaching more enjoyable, rewarding, and effective.

> **W**hen assessment is seen as a meaningful and dynamic part of working with young children, and when it is linked to the curriculum, teachers gain the true benefits of ongoing assessment.

References

Campbell, F.A., C.T. Ramey, E.P. Pungello, J. Sparling, & S. Miller-Johnson. 2002. Early childhood education: Young adult outcomes from the Abecedarian Project. *Applied Developmental Science* 6: 42–57.

Cicchetti, D., & S. Wagner. 1990. Alternative assessment strategies for the evaluation of infants and toddlers: An organizational perspective. In *Handbook of early childhood intervention,* eds. J.P. Shonkoff & S.J. Meisels. New York: Cambridge University Press.

Dodge, D.T., L.J. Colker, & C. Heroman. 2001. *The Creative Curriculum developmental continuum assessment toolkit for ages 3–5.* Washington, DC: Teaching Strategies.

Dodge, D.T., L.J. Colker, & C. Heroman. 2002. *The Creative Curriculum for Preschool*. 4th ed. Washington, DC: Teaching Strategies.

Hauser-Crane, P., & J.P. Shonkoff. 1995. Mastery motivation: Implications for intervention. In *Mastery motivation: Origins, concep-tualizations, and applications,* eds. R. MacTurk & G. Morgan, 257–72. Norwood, NJ: Ablex.

Head Start Bureau. 2001. Head Start child outcomes framework. *Head Start Bulletin* 70: 44–50.

HHS (U.S. Department of Health and Human Services). 2003. *Head Start FACES 2000: A whole-child perspective on program performance, fourth progress report.* Washington, DC: Administration for Children and Families.

IRA (International Reading Association) & NAEYC. 1998. Joint Position Statement. Learning to read and write: Developmentally appropriate practices for young children. *Young Children* 53 (4): 30–46. Online: www.naeyc.org/positionstatements/learning_readwrite.

McCune, L., B. Kalmanson, M.B. Fleck, R. Glazewski, & J. Sillari. 1990. An interdisciplinary model of infant assessment. In *Handbook of early childhood intervention,* eds. J.P Shonkoff & S.J. Meisels. New York: Cambridge University Press.

NAEYC & NAECS/SDE (National Association of Early Childhood Specialists in State Departments of Education). 2003. Joint Position Statement. Early childhood curriculum, assessment, and program evaluation: Building an effective, accountable system in programs for children birth through age 8. Online: www.naeyc.org/positionstatements/cape.

NAEYC & NCTM (National Council of Teachers of Mathematics). 2002. *Early childhood mathematics: Promoting good beginnings.* Online: www.naeyc.org/positionstatements/mathematics.

Peisner-Feinberg, E.S., M.R. Burchinal, R.M. Clifford, M.L. Culkin, C. Howes, S.L. Kagan, N. Yazejian, P. Byler, J. Rustici, & J. Zelazo. 2000. *The children of the Cost, Quality, and Outcomes Study go to school: Technical report.* Chapel Hill: University of North Carolina at Chapel Hill, Frank Porter Graham Child Development Center.

Infant/Toddler Assessment
One Program's Experience

Margo L. Dichtelmiller and Laura Ensler

A child's developmental level and cultural background can affect how she approaches assessment tasks.

Assessment of infants and toddlers in a center-based or home visiting program can be a challenging task. However, if educators are to make valid interpretations and good decisions about what to teach and how to teach it, they must assess all the children they teach, even the infants and toddlers.

This article explores developmentally appropriate assessment for infants and toddlers, recognizing the challenges involved in this endeavor and outlining the benefits that can be realized from systematic, ongoing observation and assessment. Both the challenges and the benefits are illustrated by one program's implementation of a functional assessment, the Ounce Scale (Meisels et al. 2003), a new approach that focuses on the purposes of children's behavior.

Margo L. Dichtelmiller, PhD, is an assistant professor at Eastern Michigan University in Ypsilanti. An author of *The Work Sampling System,* Margo teaches inservice and preservice teachers about infants and toddlers and early childhood assessment.

Laura Ensler, MSEd, directs an Early Head Start program in Rockaway, New York, for pregnant teens and teenage families, sponsored by Visiting Nurse Service of New York. A frequent lecturer, Laura has taught at the NYU School of Continuing Education, Bank Street College of Education, and elsewhere.

The challenges of assessing infants and toddlers

Although assessment holds great potential to help caregivers understand the children they care for, it can be challenging to assess infants and toddlers, especially if one views assessment as a one-on-one testing interaction. Babies have short attention spans, particularly if what they are being asked to do does not interest them; and they express strong feelings if a toy they are happily playing with is removed. They are strongly affected by contextual factors. If a baby is hot, cold, tired, hungry, afraid, or not interested, it is unlikely that you will get a valid assessment of his development.

In addition, a child's developmental level and cultural background can affect how she approaches assessment tasks. For example, during periods of stranger anxiety, it may be difficult for an infant to interact easily with an unfamiliar adult. Moreover, infants' and toddlers' limited language skills do not allow them to tell you what they know; instead, adults must decipher nonverbal cues, vocalizations, and body language.

Even when educators use less formal types of assessment, observing and assessing infants and toddlers in centers or on home visits can be a challenge. Infants and toddlers cannot be left to play independently, and simply finding time to observe and take notes requires a high degree of professional

commitment, as well as efficient time management skills. Very young children require ongoing attention and assistance, which means that caregivers cannot observe "out of the action" but must observe while they are interacting with the children. Moreover, because caregivers often carry infants and toddlers, taking notes is not always an option.

In the complex and ever changing environment of an infant/toddler program, it can be daunting to find the time and energy to make assessment an integral part of teaching.

Why assess infants and toddlers?

Despite the myriad challenges posed by the developmental characteristics of infants and toddlers and the busy nature of infant-toddler programs, assessment of very young children is an essential part of quality care. Careful observation of infants and toddlers on an ongoing basis, followed by sensitive interpretation of their behavior within a developmental continuum, offers many benefits to infants, toddlers, and their caregivers.

Understanding and connecting with children

Assessing infants and toddlers helps caregivers build relationships with the children (Jablon, Dombro, & Dichtelmiller 1999). The better you understand a child and take actions based on those understandings, the stronger your relationship with that child. Studying children, which is the heart of assessment, helps teachers discern why children do what they do, what makes them smile and laugh, and what tasks are difficult for them. Caregivers develop respect for the children's strengths and challenges, feel connected to them, and come to appreciate each child's individuality. These social relationships provide the foundation for learning (Vygotsky 1978).

Monitoring progress

Effective assessment allows educators to describe and track children's development over time to ensure that children are growing and developing as expected. Infants and toddlers grow and change at a rapid pace. If careful observational assessment reveals that a child is not progressing, the caregiver can seek further evaluation. When programs keep track of children's developmental progress, families can be reassured that their child is developing typically. If families have concerns about their child's development, they can share these concerns with a caregiver who has carefully monitored the child's progress.

Guiding and individualizing planning

A major reason for regularly assessing infants and toddlers is to translate the assessment information into individualized plans for children. Too often assessment is seen as ancillary to the caregiver's primary role, and assessment information sits unused in file drawers. Uncovering infants' strengths and areas of difficulty allows the caregiver to tailor interactions, routines, materials, and activities to each child's individual needs and interests. If, for example, an eight-month-old is just beginning to move around by crawling, perhaps some large, lightweight balls should be introduced so he can crawl after them. Assessing infants and toddlers can guide the processes of setting goals and planning curriculum.

Strengthening relationships and empowering families

Assessing infants and toddlers can strengthen the relationship between the home and the program and can empower families. The caregiver who regularly shares informa-

Photos © Paula Jorde Bloom

> **S**tudying children, which is the heart of assessment, **helps teachers discern why children do what they do,** what makes them smile and laugh, and what tasks are difficult for them.

tion with families and listens appreciatively to each family's stories and comments is forging a relationship of equality with the families. Partnering with families to learn about children's development acknowledges that families have unique information to share and that their perspective is valued. When family members feel that they have something valuable to share with the program, they are more likely to become involved in a meaningful way.

Task-based versus functional assessment

To realize the full benefits associated with assessment of infants and toddlers, the approach to assessment must be developmentally appropriate. Assessments of very young children have traditionally relied on a task-based or milestone approach in which infants work in a one-on-one situation with an examiner. They are presented with materials and encouraged to do certain activities. For example, a toddler may be asked to find the eyes, nose, and mouth on a doll. After this interaction the doll is removed and another toy presented. Naturally many infants and toddlers react negatively to this process; the resulting information may not be reliable or valid.

Functional assessment (Greenspan 1996; Bagnato, Neisworth, & Munson 1997; Meisels 2001) uses a different approach. Rather than trying to elicit predetermined behaviors through specific tasks, caregivers look for each child's individual way of accomplishing certain functions or purposes. For example, a caregiver might observe a child at a center or during a home visit in order to discover how the child shows trust in others, communicates, or moves around his environment.

Children accomplish these functions in many different ways, all of which are valid. Instead of looking for narrowly defined skills such as putting a cube in a cup or drawing a vertical line, the caregiver comes to appreciate the wide variety of ways that infants and toddlers show us what they know and can do. For example, one six-month-old might show her trusting relationship with her mother or caregiver by reaching out whenever that person is near; another six-month-old might smile whenever he catches the caregiver's eye; still another might make sounds to attract the caregiver's attention. All these behaviors show the existence of a trusting relationship; each behavior reflects an individual's expression influenced by development, experience, culture, and personality.

> **A caregiver might observe a child at a center or during a home visit in order to discover how the child shows trust in others, communicates, or moves around his environment.**

Needed: A new concept

To provide developmentally appropriate assessment that benefits infants and toddlers, we need a new vision of assessment: a vision of caregivers studying infants and toddlers to learn how they accomplish certain important functions—moving around, forming relationships, manipulating objects, solving problems, and communicating with others. It was this new vision that motivated an Early Head Start program to adopt a particular functional assessment, the Ounce Scale.

The Visiting Nurse Service of New York (VNSNY) operates an Early Head Start program that serves 75 pregnant and parenting teenagers and their infants and toddlers in the Rockaway region of Queens. The program provides comprehensive, integrated home- and center-based health and development services designed to (1) increase the growth and development of infants/toddlers and families; (2) enhance parent-child attachment; (3) empower parents and strengthen families through education, employment, and decision-making opportunities; and (4) strengthen relationships with community agencies to foster a safe, nurturing community environment conducive to children's development. The program's two primary methods of service delivery are a full-day, full-year, center-based program and a home visiting program. Staff members include infant/toddler teachers and home visitors, social workers, and public health nurses.

Laura Ensler, the program director, recognized a need for a systematic way to keep track of children's development that took into account the context of each child's life. In her search for a tool, she rejected task-based assessments because they relied on minimal observation of the child and often resulted in labeling very young children. After participating in the field test of the Ounce Scale, the VNSNY Early Head Start program adopted the assessment for use in its home visiting and center-based programs.

The Ounce Scale

The Ounce Scale is an observational, functional assessment created to assess children from birth through 42 months. It was designed to be used in Early Head Start programs, child care centers, Even Start programs, home visiting programs, and family child care homes. It can be used effectively with children living in poverty, children at risk or with disabilities, and children growing and developing typically.

The Ounce Scale is organized around eight age levels, and it addresses six areas of development:

Personal Connections—How children show trust

Feelings about Self—How children express who they are

Relationships with Other Children—How children act around other children

Understanding and Communicating—How children understand and communicate

Exploration and Problem Solving—How children explore and figure things out

Movement and Coordination—How children move their bodies and use their hands

These areas of development provide the framework for the caregiver's and family's observations of the child.

The Ounce Scale has three parts: the Observation Record, the Family Album, and the Developmental Profile and Standards. The Observation Record is an age-level booklet that serves as the caregiver's observation tool (Marsden, Dombro, & Dichtelmiller 2003). Questions and brief descriptions in each area of development focus the observations. Caregivers or home visitors answer each observation question by observing and recording what they see as they watch children in a variety of natural situations at home or at a center.

The Family Album is a small, brightly colored booklet, similar to a scrapbook or baby book. The album serves as the family's observational tool in which they can write notes and stories, keep photographs, and save drawings that illustrate the baby's growth and development. It also includes suggested home activities. Because the Family Album is organized

around the same observation questions as the Observation Record, families and caregivers can focus on the same questions at the same time.

The Developmental Profile and Standards is the third element of the scale. The Developmental Profile is a rating scale that evaluates children's behavior in four areas: social and emotional, communication and language, cognitive development, and physical development. At the end of each age level, the caregiver reviews the data from the Observation Record and Family Album and compares them to descriptions of expected behavior from the Developmental Profile in order to evaluate the children's development.

One program's experience

Teachers and home visitors at the VNSNY Early Head Start program found the Observation Record easy to use. Like other checklists, it provided an outline of the types of behaviors to observe. According to one teacher, this structure "empowers me as an observer and makes me feel competent about what I'm observing." Another teacher pointed to the rationales in the Observation Record as "refreshers for understanding developmental domains. The examples coax me into remembering more and thinking of more examples that I've seen."

Having access to recorded observations, organized for easy retrieval, enables teachers to feel more confident about making early intervention referrals. "[Referrals are] no longer based on a feeling or a brief screening but on actual observations collected over time." Several teachers said that using the Observation

Record enhanced their observation skills and helped them see children as individuals.

The Family Album provides families with an observational tool that acknowledges each family's unique knowledge about their child. As one caregiver said, "If we do the Family Album together with parents as partners, our relationship grows and we are able to establish trust. Doing it together removes us from the role of expert and empowers parents to become the experts about their own children."

Although the Family Album fits easily into the routine of a home visit, center-based caregivers found it to be the most challenging part of the Ounce Scale to implement. Limited time with families made it difficult to integrate the Family Album into classroom life.

The VNSNY Early Head Start program developed several strategies to increase families' use of the album in center-based classrooms. They enlisted the help of "Ounce mentors," families who had used the Family Album successfully, and asked them to show their Family Albums, introduce the album to new families, and help these families start their own albums. Classroom teachers invited families into the classroom to observe their child's activities and make notes for the Family Album. They also created an Ounce Family Bulletin Board in each classroom to display pages from Family Albums and explanatory information related to a particular area of development.

The VNSNY Early Head Start caregivers and home visitors found the Developmental Profile easy to understand and use. It gave them a chance to summarize what they knew about a child and make plans for the future. As one staff member said, "When I complete the Developmental Profile with the family, I also update the Family Partnership Agreement and review the family's goals for the child. It pulls it all together." Home visitors noted that families are more comfortable with Needs Development ratings because they have been involved in the assessment process and observed the same behaviors as the home visitor.

Home visitors and center-based caregivers agreed that using an ongoing, functional assessment provided them with a more complete picture of each child based on their own observations, as well as the family's observations over time. Some commented that observing over several months is a much different experience than administering a one-on-one, task-based assessment. "The Ounce Scale allows you to see progress over time. You don't feel locked into making evaluations of a child each day or after a short assessment. It's a way to see a child in context and over time." Caregivers translated the assessment data into curriculum planning. For example, one caregiver noted that when several of her children demonstrated a newfound love of language, she decided to introduce a new, longer, and more interesting song during circle time.

The comments from the VNSNY caregivers clearly demonstrate the benefits of using functional assessment. Not only does it more accurately measure a very young child's performance in the context of daily routines, it also empowers the family to participate in the assessment process. Because the assessment information is gathered in the child's everyday environment, it is easily translated into curriculum plans. This program's experiences show that whatever the challenges of using a functional assessment, there are significant positive impacts on the children, families, caregivers, and program.

> **Caregivers or home visitors** answer each observation question by observing and recording what they see as they watch children in **a variety of natural situations at home or at a center.**

> **B**ecause the assessment information is gathered in the child's everyday environment, it is easily translated into curriculum plans.

References

Bagnato, S.J., J.T. Neisworth, & S.M. Munson. 1997. *Linking assessment and early intervention: An authentic curriculum-based approach.* Baltimore: Paul H. Brookes.

Greenspan, S.I. 1996. Assessing the emotional and social functioning of infants and young children. In *New visions for the developmental assessment of infants and young children*, eds. S.J. Meisels & E. Fenichel, 231–66. Washington, DC: Zero to Three/National Center for Infants, Toddlers and Families.

Jablon, J.R., A.L. Dombro, & M.L. Dichtelmiller. 1999. *The power of observation.* Washington, DC: Teaching Strategies.

Marsden, D.B., A.L. Dombro, & M.L. Dichtelmiller. 2003. *The Ounce Scale user's guide.* New York: Pearson Early Learning,

Meisels, S.J. 2001. Fusing assessment and intervention: Changing parents' and providers' views of young children. Zero to Three 21 (4): 4–10.

Meisels, S.J., A.L. Dombro, D.B. Marsden, D.R. Weston, & A.M. Jewkes. 2003. *The Ounce Scale.* New York: Pearson Early Learning.

Vygotsky, L.S. 1978. *Mind in society: The development of higher psychological processes.* Cambridge, MA: Harvard University Press.

From Policing to Participation

Overturning the Rules and Creating Amiable Classrooms

Carol Anne Wien

We were playing outside after a rainy day, and there was a huge mud puddle the size of a large table and of course a rule about no playing in the mud—children get dirty. The children played around the perimeter of the puddle, digging with shovels and throwing rocks in and watching them splash. Then some started tapping their toes in the water. We thought, "Well that's OK, they're wearing boots." Then they were up to their ankles in water. We were really hesitant but thought, "What's the big deal? It's only mud." But then we were anxious: "They are going to be really dirty; what will the parents say?" Before we knew it, children were jumping off the bench into the mud puddle, tumbling over each other. They were covered in mud. We were all standing back, kind of white-knuckling it and thinking, "Oh, should we let them?" We decided yes, and went to get the camera.

How did the staff of three child care centers transform their work lives from continuous policing and correction of young children to a pedagogy in which they and the children participate together in constructing richly lived events? How were they able to let children engage in such wild activities as playing in a fresh mud puddle? Their experience shows that, contrary to common sense, aggression, accidents, and the stress of constantly enforcing rules are all reduced and transformed when many rules are eliminated by staff in a collaborative process.

The process of reexamining and then removing multiple rules for children's behavior permitted fuller participation in the life of the centers and led to an overall transformation of power relationships: both teachers and children gained more power to affect what happened in the programs. While reexamining the rules was not the only thoughtful process undertaken by the teachers, it seemed to be especially powerful in opening up practice toward more expansive living. Simultaneously, teachers reexamined the physical environments (organization of time and space) and the ways these contributed to a stressful atmosphere

---

Four early childhood educators and two professors took part in the discussions that form the basis for this article:

Carol Anne Wien, PhD, is an associate professor in the Faculty of Education at York University in Toronto, Canada. She is the author of a forthcoming book, *Early Childhood Teachers Negotiating Standardized Curriculum,* from Teachers College Press.

Karyn Callaghan, ECE,C, MEd, is a professor of early childhood education at Mohawk College in Hamilton, Ontario, and originator/coordinator of the Artists at the Centre project, which brings artists to centers exploring the Reggio Emilia approach.

Bobbie-Jo Gramigna, ECE,C, is supervisor at Templemead Umbrella Family and Child Centers in Hamilton, Ontario. She previously taught at a workplace child care center and was a mentor to colleagues sharing an interest in Reggio Emilia.

Brenda Gardiner, ECE,C, is assistant director and head preschool teacher at McMaster Children's Center in Hamilton, Ontario, which began exploring the Reggio approach in 1999 and joined Artists at the Centre.

Laurie Jeandron, ECE,C, is an instructor in early childhood education at Mohawk College in Hamilton, Ontario. As former supervisor of Scott Park Children's Centre, she collaborated with a team to create an environment to support children's interests.

Melita Veinotte, ECE,C, RT, is an early childhood educator at Templemead Umbrella Family and Child Centers in Hamilton, Ontario. She taught at Scott Park Children's Center when it began to explore the Reggio approach.

This research was supported by the Hamilton Community Foundation. For more information on the Artists at the Centre project, visit www.artistsatthecentre.ca.

that generated aggression. As Karyn Callaghan comments, "The whole question of letting go of power just flies in the face of [established] practice."

The children and families served

The three centers are all nonprofit sites—one with 63 children on a university campus, one (42 children) in a workplace setting, and the other (32 children) in a high school. In the last, eight children have special needs and another 16 are considered to have general developmental delays. All three centers are inclusive settings with resource-teacher consultants for children with special needs. Staff are qualified early childhood educators, and the centers accept early childhood education students in practicum placements. As an example of diversity, in one center 40 percent of the families served use English as a second language in their homes, with 10 percent being newly arrived immigrants. Cultures and languages of the families include Mandarin and its dialects, as well as Spanish and Portuguese. The centers serve many single-parent families and families with two parents on shift work.

Established practice in the centers

In all three centers the established, conventional practice was rule based, yet staff thought they had few rules and no problems as a result. Safety for young children was the highest priority, with rules often designed to prevent harm to children. However, in creating the rules the educators did not consider the possibility that harm might come to the children and teachers in other ways as a consequence of these rules. Callaghan noted, "Safety, you can justify any rule with safety."

Another justification was government requirements, that is, the authority of the official regulating body. Sometimes these regulations were real; sometimes they were assumed to exist by the teachers but in fact did not. Teacher anxiety over responsibility for young children's lives is clear. Rules proliferated out of fear for the safety of the young and vulnerable charges.

Bobbie-Jo described how her center had been "very structured." For example, "we had pictures of three faces" defining how many children were permitted in a location, and "children were not allowed to take toys [from one play area to another]." Brenda, at another center, said, "You always had to go down the slide feet

first, and you always had to sit up going down the slide." Laurie noted that in the center serving many children with special needs, staff were "stopping things from happening all day long." For instance, only four children were allowed in the water play area, so any additional children who tried to join the play would be redirected to another activity.

With tightly defined spaces for every activity, teachers acted as traffic officers, directing children to available spots. The time segments for activities were brief, play spaces rigorously defined, and play areas small and tight. In one center, for instance, two separate playrooms each had precisely the same interest areas, all of them small.

To give an idea of the tone at the centers during their rule-governed regimes, here is a partial list of what children could and could not do. One center discovered they had 26 rules for outdoor play, including this sampling:

> No swinging from the slide.
> No crashing riding toys.
> Only run in one direction.
> No sitting on balls.
> No using big brooms.
> No banging on the shed.
> No licking the door.

Another center found that it had many indoor rules, including such specifics as the order for eating lunch and other rules such as

> No blowing on food.
> No other toys used with playdough.
> No toys traveling around the room from area to area.
> Sit in the same seat for lunch every day.

When I asked the educators to define a *rule* in such practice, Melita said, "Something necessary to keep control."

"And control is conceived as?"

Several teachers responded, "Children obeying, children doing as they are told."

Brenda added, "It was a comfort for teachers to know there was a rule in place and everything would run smoothly."

"Ah, you believed that this control would in fact work! [*chorus of yeses*] But in fact it didn't, because people were policing all the time!"

The amount of energy teachers spent on enforcing the rules to govern the children was immense and highly stressful. Laurie said, "The energy the staff were expending on policing the center, redirecting children, and giving time-out was just so draining." She described the block area at her center:

> Children would go in, and things would start flying, blocks would get knocked over, kids would get pushed, and there would be yelling and screaming. Half the time you would not want the block center open because you couldn't deal with it. It was so loud. That whole half of the room would get really crazy. The noise level would go up, and then children would start bouncing off each other and teachers would start pulling out their hair. You could make a comedy movie of it.

Reexamining the rules

How did changes to practice begin? Callaghan offered workshops for the early childhood community in which the match between values and practices was examined. Influenced by interpretations of the Reggio Emilia approach (Malaguzzi 1996; Cadwell 1997; Hendrick 1997; Edwards, Gandini, & Forman 1998), she invited teachers to explore their images of children, and she gently questioned some scenarios observed in the community, such as

> Children told what position to lie in on their cots.
> No toys allowed from home.
> Weekly themes planned for the entire year without considering children's interests.

Callaghan asked, "If we believe that children are unique and to be respected, and yet we are making children finish all the food on their plates before they get to have a drink, or there are designated times when they can go to the washroom, then what must the view really be?" The notion of a regulated child forced to follow prescribed institutional scripts for living had not occurred to those attending the workshop.

The invitation to consider the contrast between the rule-based scenarios seen in their centers and the lovely images of children to which the teachers gave lip service prompted Bobbie-Jo to challenge teachers at her center to rethink their rules. This process was difficult. When they tried to discuss their rules as a group, individuals reacted so strongly to one another's rules, laughing and making faces, that they had to make a rule not to be judgmental about rules. The

> **The amount of energy teachers spent on enforcing the rules to govern the children was immense and highly stressful.**

teachers described so many rules that the group could not deal with all of them in one session.

A decision to have a second meeting with a focus on one area only—outdoor play—allowed the staff to note 26 teacher-generated rules for children's play. This was many more than they *thought* they had, but these rules had never been written down. Bobbie-Jo noted, "Individually we had only a few rules, but when you put all those rules together, for a child there were a lot of different rules because staff had different expectations."

Collaboratively, the teachers decided on three criteria for a rule: Did [the behavior targeted by the rule] harm the child? Did it harm others? Did it damage property? With the criteria in mind, the group began to examine the rules. Someone noticed that play areas were closed when parents picked up children. Did this rule meet the criteria? No. The teachers asked, "So why do we have that area closed?"

Applying the criteria to their rules opened up the process of discarding rules. On the outdoor playground, for example, the 26 rules were reduced to five:

> Riding toys are for riding.
> Riding toys stay off the climber.
> Sand in the sandbox.
> Safe bike riding.
> Hockey sticks stay down.

Bobbie-Jo provided an example of the process of questioning that could lead to rule reduction. One day a child brought in a new action figure and told Bobbie-Jo about it. A teacher interrupted, saying, "That needs to go in his cubby."

"Wait a minute. Why?"

"Because it's not his show-and-tell day."

"Let's put this in adult perspective. Suppose on the weekend you got engaged. You come in with your engagement ring and want to show everybody, and I say to you, 'Whoa, whoa, it's not your day. But you can put that in your locker.' It's the same thing."

"OK, he can keep it in here [the classroom], as long as he shares it with everybody."

"I can go along with that as long as I can have a turn with your jewelry when you're done."

Bobbie-Jo argued that there are many toys to share in centers but "not everything is for sharing." "If it's not OK for me to borrow another adult's jewelry, watch, or sweater, I don't think it's OK for us to expect children to share their things."

Teachers worried that welcoming play materials from home would not work, and they called Bobbie-Jo to come and see how upset children were the first few times such toys were brought into class. Gradually, it became easier to permit items from home to be part of classroom life. Melita said, "It really reduced stress. You are not in power struggles with children." Brenda added that "parents really appreciate it too," not having to struggle over telling a child to leave a precious item behind. Children's self-investment in their belongings shows an attachment to their identity, and separating from something that contributes to identity is emotionally difficult.

Two months after the initial workshop, Bobbie-Jo, the first to stimulate a reexamination of rules in her center, presented the experience at a local teacher network meeting. After handing out a revised list of new and reduced rules, Bobbie-Jo said, "They thought it was completely crazy. They said, 'I would like to see you come and do that at our center!'" Removing rules seemed counterintuitive.

Laurie said of her center, "We started to abandon the rules and then understood their impact on both children and teachers. We were dealing with 'behavior' on a regular basis. We asked ourselves, 'Why are we doing this? Why are only four children allowed in water play? How is that promoting children's development?'"

The teachers began allowing as many children as wished to to come to the water play area and found that the focus of the teachers became one of negotiating and developing children's social skills for entering play. The teachers made the water table more accessible, pulling it away from the wall so children could crowd all around it. The playdough table too went from having three places to many places. The staff focus became "giving children the skills to enter the situation," such as problem-solving how to find another place to play.

Overall, the teachers in all three centers found that eliminating rules reduced stress. In addition, Callaghan was struck by the process of *negotiating* rules when incidents arose, with teachers asking each other, "What do you think about this?" Children were invited to join the discussions when teachers asked,

> **We asked ourselves, "Why are we doing this? Why are only four children allowed in water play? How is that promoting children's development?"**

ASSESSMENT

"Do we need a rule about this?" Of interest is the fact that the changes and their consequences were consistent across the three centers and that the changes appeared quickly, over months, not years.

Changes in the physical environments

Reducing the rules in a setting, and experiencing positive change as a result, also led to explorations of the organization of the physical environment. Laurie described how the aforementioned block area in her center was reorganized and enlarged (from 4 by 6 feet to 10 by 20 feet) with much better results for the children. Teachers also found ways to permit block structures to remain standing, rather than insisting on tidying up each day, so children could return later and continue building. This meant redesigning the layout for cots at naptime, but teachers did this now that their priority was children's activity rather than adult convenience. The impact of the change astonished the teachers. Laurie noted,

> The mania in the block area just started to die down. Children began to interact in a much nicer way. There was less fighting because there was more room. Children were not bumping into each other.
>
> There were more materials available. There were fewer rules about what you could and couldn't do, and therefore the teachers, instead of having to stand over the children and police them, could go in and participate. They could build with the children. They could draw, take photographs, go get other materials. There was a lot more spontaneous interaction.

Surprisingly, it was also much quieter. In addition, teachers in this center found the incidence of accidents and aggression decreasing. A government requirement calls for all centers to complete accident reports for any injuries. One year, among 12 children there were 42 injury incidents—33 accidental and 9 due to aggression (hitting, spitting, biting, tripping, and so forth). The next year, after the center had reduced its rules, incidents were reduced considerably among the same 12 children, with aggressive acts down by 50 percent. Total incidents were 25, of which 21 were due to accidents, four to aggression. While many factors affect accident rates, the teachers' perception was that the reduction resulted from the changes in pedagogy. This was both remarkable to them and corroborated their sense that the changes they made resulted in much more positive environments for children. The entire emotional tone of their center is more positive.

Teachers' priority was children's activity rather than adult convenience.

Many things were happening simultaneously. The examination of rules, teachers' surprise at their numbers, and the subsequent reduction created new degrees of freedom for both children and teachers to act spontaneously. This process stood out as momentous in its impact on changing practice. Other changes included a softening of the environment, such as creating conversation areas, adding Monet prints and flowers to bathrooms, and inviting parents to contribute family photos. Brenda said, "I love the fact that each of the three centers is different."

Consequences of changes in pedagogy for the children

The biggest effect of rule reduction was that settings became quieter and calmer, with less fuss about enforcing minor rules. With less monitoring to do and calmer children, staff could participate more fully, engaging with children in their activities. The teachers developed greater interest in following the children's lead, such as permitting them to interact fully and vigorously with a mud puddle in springtime.

Brenda made a videotape showing children deeply engaged in block play, woodworking, play with Legos, and dramatic play in the loft. Half an hour into the video, children are still playing in the same areas. Laurie commented, "When children made their own choices, the time spent at activities increased." Concentration spans for self-initiated activity became long and sustained.

The children began to generate their own rules and to involve themselves

© Sylvie Wickstrom

in self-governing, a process Vygotsky long ago showed as necessary to the development of will power (1976; [1930–1935] 1978). For example, at Bobbie-Jo's center a group of boys made a space for hockey on the small playground, with rules about how to swing the hockey stick ("Not off the ground"). They made a net and demarcated their area with pylons. Such opportunities to generate rules for group activities make people feel they belong to the social group. Feelings of belonging are essential to any notion of community, and to the commitment of members to that community.

From rule- and clock-driven practice to values-based, responsive pedagogy

The teachers felt several things happened simultaneously. As they let go and gave more control to the children, the children learned that the adults thought of them as capable. By reorganizing the environments into more expansive spaces and reducing the number of rules, staff began to see new possibilities for practice. Several teachers joked about their previous focus on time and efficiency: "I remember always looking at the clock, thinking, 'OK, let's go, let's go' *[laughing];* how many kids can you get to pee in five minutes?"

Previously, children were lucky if they had 15 or 20 minutes in an area. It was often 20 minutes of play, 5 minutes of tidying up, 5 minutes of transition, and then play in a new area. A teacher noted, "Time was a rule." Time was a rule that could not be broken. Time as a production schedule, and teachers as keepers of the schedule (Wien 1995), produced policing to maintain the schedule. With the changes in stance, practice was more relaxed, less clock driven.

Callaghan saw teachers taking ownership of their practice. They wondered, "What do I like?" and "What's driving me crazy?" and saw possibilities for changing to practices that they preferred, chose, and assessed for themselves. We might say the teachers removed themselves from the established scripts for institutional routine and were inventing practice to fit their own contexts.

All the teachers found that the changes reduced stress. The energy of policing, correcting, and giving time-out was exhausting for teachers; it created negative energy, tearing at the emotional well-being of staff and children. Laurie said, "That energy is now turned into facilitating social interaction among children, exploring their interests, and actually talking to children." With staff chatting with and observing children more, the children are receiving more positive attention and, according to the teachers, "there are fewer behavior problems to deal with."

The teachers have noticed increased calm among the children and a sense of emotional satisfaction. For example, after the vigorous mud-puddle play, the wet and dirty children had to be cleaned up, and their clothes washed and dried before parents arrived. Melita said: "It was the calmest, most easygoing change and cleanup ever. I couldn't believe it. They sat and helped each other. It was amazing, and we noticed that, as we were right in the middle of it."

Resistance to change

All the teachers note the role of resistance in the process of change. Laurie said, "When I entered practice in 1984 or '85, I was very much a controlling sort of teacher. I was very consistent, [thinking] this is the fastest, most convenient way we could get it all done." She added that after the radical change in her practice, it was interesting to look back on the way she had been. The teachers agreed that it is difficult to think there are better ways to function as early childhood educators.

Bobbie-Jo commented that when she began as supervisor, one teacher said, "You're that Reggio girl, and don't think for a minute you are going to do that here!" Whatever interpretations people make of the term *Reggio,* advocates of the Reggio approach note that they first create their practice out of whatever provocations stimulate a sense of ownership and participation in their own teaching. "Of course we're not going to force you to do anything," Bobbie-Jo responded to the teacher and proceeded to talk with staff about their view of children and what they wished to see in the center. She described how an especially resistant staff person was later overheard telling visiting teachers the results of following the children's lead: "I can't believe what a difference this has made. I am no longer stressed when I go home."

Teachers taking ownership of their teaching practice

What happened and how did it happen? From the teacher educator's perspective, Callaghan believes a crucial moment in changing practice was beginning with teachers' images of children. "To start with the view of the child is pivotal." Making explicit this positive image of children permits a conscious investigation of whether the pedagogy of teachers supports their images of children. When teachers see mismatches between their newly explicit image of what children can do and their teaching practices, they begin to see openings for doing something differently that better honors their values.

Once the reexamination of established practice had begun, possibilities for teachers' participation in creating their own pedagogy opened up. Teachers asked, "Do you think we could _____?" or "What's possible?" Bobbie-Jo noted that "the adults are doing exactly what we are doing with the children. We are asking the children, 'What are the possibilities on this? What can happen? Make your theories. Let's try it out. Let's revisit that.'"

What has happened is a change in teacher stance. There is a new disposition to think in terms of possibilities, to invent in response to context—an aspect of good constructivist teaching (Forman 2002). Laurie commented that this change requires redefining what it means to be a good teacher and that expectations for job performance also have to change.

These teachers are no longer "keepers of the routine" (Wien 1995), programming according to the production schedule, but partners with children. If teachers take control of their own practice, and of assessing the match between their values and their pedagogy, then teaching becomes not performing a job to someone else's criteria, but instead living in responsiveness to children and families and sharing a broad sense of possibilities about all the ways to participate together. Something about the change is profoundly democratic, if democracy is conceived as full creative participation of all members of the community.

Conclusion

The emotional tone of the three centers has changed from surveillance in order to enforce the rules and schedule to one of positive, even joyful, participation. There is a release of energy, a "raising of windhorse" (to borrow a phrase of the Shambhala Buddhists)—a new, positive energy. Callaghan says, "You can taste it when you walk into a center. You just feel there is this life there." Bobbie-Jo adds, "You can feel it, the energy rising; it is just so exciting."

Vecchi (2002, 56) reminds us of Gregory Bateson's phrase, "the pulsing of life," as one element relates to another and both change in response. Part of what makes rising energy so exciting is that the changes are occurring collaboratively for the group. Callaghan describes the changes as occurring "within the context of a real community of learners. We were coming together regularly and sharing these stories, bringing in documentation, bringing these lists of rules, and there was a fabulous sharing in the community."

There are now three more centers in their second year of reorganizing their practice, and six others have joined the project to begin the work. In her former practice, Brenda notes, she "couldn't wait to get out at the end of the day," whereas "working this [new] way is like being on vacation."

References

Cadwell, L. 1997. *Bringing Reggio Emilia home: An innovative approach to early childhood education.* New York: Teachers College Press.

Edwards, C., L. Gandini, & G. Forman, eds. 1998. *The hundred languages of children: The Reggio Emilia approach to early childhood education—Advanced reflections.* Rev. ed. Greenwich, CT: Ablex.

Forman, G. 2002. Constructivist teaching. Presentation at the conference of the Canadian Association for Young Children, Montreal.

Hendrick, J., ed. 1997. *First steps toward teaching the Reggio way.* Upper Saddle River, NJ: Prentice Hall.

Malaguzzi, L., ed. 1996. *The hundred languages of children: Narrative of the possible.* Catalogue to the exhibit. Reggio Emilia, Italy: Reggio Children.

Vecchi, V. 2002. *Theater curtain.* Reggio Emilia, Italy: Reggio Children.

Vygotsky, L. 1976. The role of play in development. In *Play—Its role in development and evolution,* eds J. Bruner, A. Jolly, & K. Sylva. New York: Penguin.

Vygotsky, L.S. [1930–1935] 1978. *Mind in society: The development of higher psychological processes,* eds. and trans. M. Cole, V. John-Steiner, S. Scribner, & E. Souberman. Cambridge, MA: Harvard University Press.

Wien, C.A. 1995. *Developmentally appropriate practice in "real life": Stories of teacher practical knowledge.* New York: Teachers College Press.

RESEARCH IN REVIEW

School Readiness Assessment

Kelly L. Maxwell and Richard M. Clifford

Kelly L. Maxwell, PhD, is a scientist at the Frank Porter Graham (FPG) Child Development Institute and codirector of the National Prekindergarten Center, University of North Carolina at Chapel Hill. She has directed several large-scale studies of young children, including a statewide study of readiness for school in North Carolina.

Richard M. Clifford, PhD, is a senior scientist at the FPG Child Development Institute and codirector of both the National Center for Early Development and Learning and the National Prekindergarten Center, University of North Carolina at Chapel Hill. He is a past president of NAEYC and is well known for his work in assessment of learning environments as well as research on the impact of programs on children's development.

Research in Review is a regular series of articles appearing in *Young Children*. This article was edited by **Diane M. Horm,** PhD, professor and director of the University of Rhode Island Child Development Centers, Department of Human Development and Family Studies, in Kingston.

School readiness assessment is a hot topic these days, in large part because of increased accountability pressures in both the public schools and early care and education settings. What exactly is meant by the phrase *school readiness assessment* and what should early care and education teachers and administrators know about it? This Research in Review article uses a question-and-answer format to address several issues about school readiness.

What is school readiness?

School readiness is about more than just children. School readiness, in the broadest sense, involves children, families, early environments, schools, and communities (NASBE 1991). Children are not innately *ready* or *not ready* for school. Their skills and development are strongly influenced by their families and through their interactions with other people and environments before coming to school. With 81 percent of U.S. children in nonparental care arrangements the year before kindergarten (West, Denton, & Germino-Hausken 2000), child care centers and family child care homes are important early environments that affect children's development and learning.

Schools are also an important piece of the readiness puzzle because different schools have different expectations about readiness. The same child, with the same strengths and needs, can be considered ready in one school and not ready in another school. It is the school's responsibility to educate all children who are old enough to legally attend school, regardless of their skills (see "Characteristics of Ready Schools," p. 30).

Finally, communities are important because readiness for school success is a community responsibility, not just the responsibility of parents and preschool teachers. Communities, for example, should provide high-quality health care and support services for families of young children and work to ensure that all families with young children have access to high-quality care and education.

Characteristics of Ready Schools

The National Education Goals Panel identifies 10 keys to schools being ready for children. Ready schools should

1. Smooth the transition between home and school.
2. Strive for continuity between early care and education programs and elementary schools.
3. Help children learn and make sense of their world.
4. Make a commitment to every child's success.
5. Show they are committed to every teacher's success.
6. Introduce and expand strategies that have been shown to improve achievement.
7. Function as learning organizations that change their practices if they do not help children.
8. Serve children in communities.
9. Take responsibility for results.
10. Maintain strong leadership.

Adapted from Rima Shore, *Ready Schools: A Report of the Goal 1 Ready Schools Resource Group* (Washington, DC: National Education Goals Panel, 1998), 5.

Most school readiness assessments focus on one part of the puzzle—the child. The National Education Goals Panel (NEGP) identifies five domains of children's development and learning that are important to school success: physical well-being and motor development, social and emotional development, approaches toward learning, language development, and cognition and general knowledge (Kagan, Moore, & Bredekamp 1995; see NEGP 1997 for a family-friendly description of school readiness). NEGP's work on school readiness has been important in broadening people's understanding of readiness beyond the ABCs and 123s and highlighting the interconnections among the five domains.

What can we learn from school readiness assessment?

School readiness assessment typically refers to assessment of young children around school entry—right before kindergarten, at kindergarten entry, or very early in the kindergarten year. The tools described as school readiness assessments vary in their purposes and designs. Thus, people using the phrase "school readiness assessment" may be referring to very different kinds of assessment.

The NEGP report *Principles and Recommendations for Early Childhood Assessments* (Shepard, Kagan, & Wurtz 1998) identifies and describes five major purposes for assessing young children. School readiness assessments typically fall under one of these purposes. It is important to understand the different purposes of assessment because assessment tools are typically developed for a single purpose and cannot easily be used for some other purpose. Each of the five purposes described in the *Principles and Recommendations* report are highlighted on the following pages.

1. Improve learning. Teachers of young children assess children's skills to help teachers adapt their teaching. The information is gathered on all children because the teacher needs to know the strengths and needs of each child in the class, not just some. Assessments are often informal, such as teacher observations or children's work samples, but may also include more formal assessments. The content of assessments for this purpose should be closely tied to the classroom curriculum.

These assessments can help kindergarten teachers improve classroom instruction by indicating children's strengths and weaknesses. Well-prepared teachers assess children's skills throughout the day, for example, by taking a picture of a child's block struc-

> **It is a school's responsibility to educate all children who are old enough to legally attend school, regardless of their skills.**

ture or writing a note at the end of the day about two children's social interaction. Focusing on school readiness assessment for the purpose of improving learning can support good teaching practices. These assessments also help families to better understand the developmental status of their children.

2. Identify children with special needs. This type of assessment generally uses a two-step process. First, all children are screened. If the screening suggests that a child's development is atypical, then the second step is implemented—the child is referred for a more thorough assessment to determine specific needs and eligibility for special education or related services. More thorough assessments must meet high standards of technical adequacy because they will be used to help make important decisions about children.

Many early care and education programs and public schools routinely conduct screenings of young children when they enter the program. Screening tools should cover general developmental milestones in multiple areas, rather than be tied specifically to a curriculum. The reason is that screening serves to determine whether a child's development is within the range of what is expected for children that age, not whether the child is learning particular concepts covered in a curriculum. Screening tools can tell parents, teachers, and specialists whether a child's development is within the range of expectations or whether the child should be referred for a more in-depth evaluation. Screenings, however, cannot positively identify children with special needs.

3. Evaluate programs. Assessments of young children's skills are often included in evaluations to determine the effectiveness of early childhood programs. Assessments chosen for this purpose should reflect program goals and be appropriate for the

> **Note**
> Although most school readiness assessments focus only on children's skills, a few states, like North Carolina, also include schools in their official definitions and assessments of school readiness (North Carolina Ready for School Goal Team 2000; Maxwell et al. 2001).

children attending the program. Generally, child assessments for the purpose of program evaluation need only include a sample of children rather than all. Program effectiveness can be determined by showing that a representative group of children from the program has improved; the program does not have to demonstrate success for each and every child. Gathering evaluation data on a sample of children rather than all children minimizes the likelihood of information being used inappropriately to make decisions about individual children or judgments about individual teachers.

School readiness assessments for program evaluation provide important indicators of an early childhood program's effectiveness in preparing children for school. They provide useful feedback to help administrators continuously improve program quality. If teachers complete these assessments, there must be safeguards to ensure that the data are not biased because the teachers are invested in the results (that is, want children in their class or program to do well). Assessments for the purpose of measuring program success typically cannot provide teachers with information to help improve children's learning. Such assessments often sample only some, not all, children, and the tools used often are not designed for the purpose of improving instruction.

4. Monitor trends over time. Communities or states may choose to conduct school readiness assessments to provide a snapshot of children as they enter kindergarten. Were this snapshot taken of a group of kindergartners every few years, then policy makers could monitor readiness trends (for example, determine whether over time children come to school with more skills). This type of school readiness assessment is broader than that done for program evaluation purposes. It does not focus on a single program but instead allows the public and policy makers to determine whether the many early childhood investments collectively are positively affecting school readiness.

As with program evaluation, child assessments for determining a ready school generally should be conducted on only a sample of children. Such assessments can provide a general picture of the characteristics of a group of children as they enter kindergarten but cannot relate information about individual children's skills. Program assessments rarely provide detail about any individual program's effectiveness. (See Love, Aber, & Brooks-Gunn 1994 for a discussion of community school readiness assessments and Scott-Little, Kagan, & Clifford 2003 for a discussion of state school readiness assessments.)

5. Use for high-stakes accountability. Assessments become high stakes if used to make decisions about individual children or teachers. Assessment tools for this purpose must meet rigorous standards of technical accuracy because they will be used to make important decisions about individuals. Because few assessment tools for young children meet high standards, the NEGP report (Shepard, Kagan, & Wurtz 1998) recommends that no child assessments be conducted for high-stakes accountability purposes until third grade.

Assessments of all children, for any purpose, may be used for high-stakes accountability. Once data are gathered and available, it may be tempting to use them to make decisions about individual children and teachers. For example, readiness assessments may be used to deny or discourage entry into kindergarten even when children are legally entitled to the service. Similarly, such assessments may be used to punish teachers whose average classroom assessment scores are low, even though the assessment tool did not meet high standards of technical adequacy. The potential risk for harm must be considered *before* any assessment data are collected. Safeguards should always be in place to minimize risks.

What characteristics of children are related to school readiness?

As stated earlier, individual children vary widely in their skills. However, research has shown that there are some general group differences in children's school readiness skills. The most recent and comprehensive national data about children's skills when they enter kindergarten come from the Early Childhood Longitudinal Study, Kindergarten Cohort (ECLS-K)—a study of a nationally representative group of approximately 22,000 kindergartners conducted by the U.S. Department

of Education (Zill & West 2001). Relevant findings from this study are highlighted below.

Family background characteristics. The ECLS-K study demonstrates that children with particular risk factors—living in a family that receives food stamps or temporary assistance; living in a single-parent home; having a mother with less than a high school education; and having parents whose primary language is not English—had lower skills when they entered school (Zill & West 2001). Specifically, children with at least one of the four risk factors had lower skills in reading, math, and general knowledge, and were more likely to be in poorer health upon entering kindergarten compared to children with no risk factors. The effect of risk factors was cumulative: children with more risk factors had lower skills in all five areas of development tested (physical well-being and motor development, social and emotional development, approaches toward learning, language development, and cognitive development and general knowledge) as they entered school.

Ethnicity. Using data from the same national study of children entering kindergarten, Lee and Burkam (2002) found that African American, Hispanic, and other children (including biracial and Native American) had lower math and reading skills at the beginning of kindergarten than did White or Asian children. African American and Hispanic children in families from lower socio-economic status had the lowest math and reading skills.

Gender. Zill and West (2001) found that girls in the ECLS-K study had slightly higher reading skills than boys, were about the same as boys in math and general knowledge, had better prosocial skills than boys, and were less likely to engage in problem behaviors than boys at the beginning of kindergarten.

These research findings suggest that some groups of children tend to start school less prepared to succeed than others. It is important to remember that these are *group* differences. Not all children within the at-risk groups had poor skills when they entered school (Zill & West 2001). Some children within each at-risk group had strong skills. Understanding group differences may help early childhood and kindergarten teachers plan appropriate learning opportunities needed for children at risk. Teachers must not make assumptions, however, about individual children's skills based on their membership in one or more of the groups discussed.

What are the limitations of school readiness assessments?

There are several important limitations of school readiness assessments. First, each assessment tool is designed for *a particular purpose* and cannot automatically or easily be used for another purpose. This means that the purpose of the assessment must be clear before an appropriate assessment tool can be selected. It also means that multiple assessment tools or approaches are needed to address multiple purposes.

Second, each school readiness assessment tool is designed with an explicit or implicit definition of school readiness. Assessment users must articulate their own definition of school readiness before they can select an appropriate measure that matches their definition. If this is not done, then the assessment instrument(s) will by default define school readiness—for better or for worse. For instance, if school readiness is defined as covering all five domains described by NEGP, then the school readiness assessment needs to measure all five domains. If the assessment measures only early literacy, then users are automatically equating readiness with literacy skills.

Third, assessments are only as good as the people conducting them. Any assessment requires careful training before use. If assessments are not done well, then the data collected may not provide the information sought. This, in turn, could lead to worse—not better—decisions being made about young children and programs.

> **The purpose of the assessment must be clear** before an appropriate assessment tool can be selected. Multiple assessment tools or approaches are needed to address multiple purposes.

ASSESSMENT 33

How should I choose a school readiness assessment?

A team of people, rather than one individual, generally works together to plan a school readiness assessment. Ideally, this team includes administrators, teachers, families, and experts in the assessment of young children's skills. The following key questions can help guide the team's planning.

• What is your definition of school readiness? Are you interested in all five domains of development—physical well-being and motor development, social and emotional development, approaches toward learning, language development, and cognitive development and general knowledge? If so, do you already collect information on some domains (for example, health), or are you looking for assessment tools that cover all five domains? If the purpose of the assessment is to improve learning, does the content of the assessment match the curriculum content?

• What is your purpose or purposes? You will need to select an assessment tool or tools to match each of your purposes.

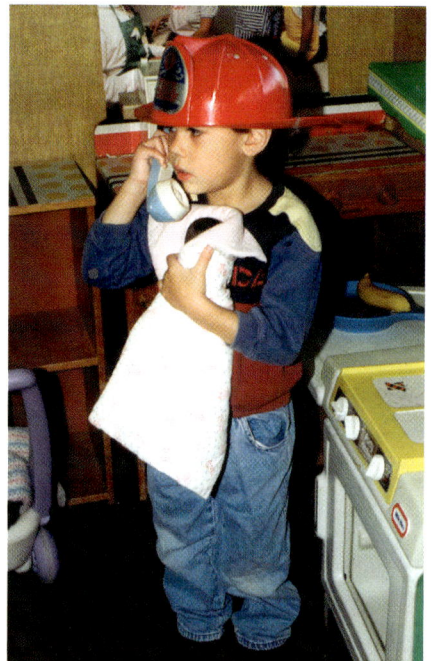

• What are the characteristics of the children to be assessed? How old are they? What languages do they speak? What are their races or ethnicities? Do some have disabilities? In what part of the country do they live? The assessment tools selected should be designed to be used with children similar to the ones you will be assessing. Furthermore, the assessment tool should include documented evidence of the characteristics of children on which the assessment was tested.

• What are the technical properties of the assessment? Is there evidence for adequate validity (the tool really measures what it claims to measure)? Is there evidence for adequate reliability (i.e., the tool produces similar results for a child, across a short time frame or across the different individuals administering the assessment)? Different purposes require different standards of technical properties (Shepard, Kagan, & Wurtz 1998).

Assessment tools for the purposes of program evaluation and monitoring trends must meet high standards for technical properties. The *Standards for Educational and Psychological Testing* (AERA, APA, & NCME Joint Committee 1999) may be a useful resource for evaluating the technical adequacy of assessments.

What are appropriate tools for conducting school readiness assessments? Who should gather school readiness assessment data?

There is no one best approach to or tool for assessing school readiness. Different purposes require different approaches. Even within a particular purpose, there is still variability in the assessments chosen. For example, a review of state prekindergarten evaluation reports identified 42 different assessment tools used in 13 state evaluations (Gilliam & Zigler 2001). For a review of commercially available school readiness assessments, see *Assessing Kindergarten Children: A Compendium of Assessment Instruments* (Niemeyer & Scott-Little 2001).

Generally, there are two different kinds of school readiness assessments: naturalistic assessments (sometimes referred to as informal or authentic) and standardized, norm-referenced assessments (sometimes referred to as formal). Naturalistic assessments include observations, work samples, and teacher checklists. Although both types of assessment are sometimes used for various purposes, the naturalistic type is most often used for the purpose of improving learning.

Standardized, norm-referenced assessments follow a standard set of administration rules so that each child theoretically experiences the assessment similarly (for example, each person administering the test gives the same instructions). Norm-referenced assessments permit a child's performance to be compared to those of other children his age. This type of assessment is used frequently for identifying children with special needs, for evaluating programs, and in high-stakes accountability. The table on page 35 highlights key advantages and disadvantages of each type of assessment.

With regard to gathering assessment information and from whom, generally it is best to tap multiple sources—teachers, families, and the child himself (Shepard, Kagan, & Wurtz 1998). In North Carolina's statewide school readiness assessment, for instance, teachers provided information about children's social skills and problem behaviors, families contributed knowledge

Types of Assessment

	Naturalistic	Standardized, norm-referenced
Advantages	• Does not disrupt a child's ongoing routine • A child has multiple chances to demonstrate skill • If done over time, it may more accurately reflect a child's skills	• Allows comparisons of same-age children • Better agreement across multiple teachers or observers • Less chance for observer/teacher bias to affect assessment results
Disadvantages	• Does not typically allow comparisons of same-age children • Hard to achieve agreement across multiple teachers or observers because each may have different understandings of the assessment items • Observer/teacher bias may affect assessment results if individuals know that the results will be used to make decisions about them or their programs • May not be as accurate for determining group comparisons or program effects • Typically requires more of the teacher's time	• May not accurately reflect skills for individual children because it is usually conducted outside the natural environment • A child is given only one opportunity to demonstrate skill • A child's performance may be less accurate if the person administering the assessment is unfamiliar to the child • Typically provides less information of use in guiding instruction for individual children • Available measures may not accurately reflect the skills of children from diverse backgrounds and of children who do not speak English

about children's health and their approaches toward learning, and one-on-one assessments conducted with children added to the learning about children's communication skills and general knowledge (Maxwell et al. 2001). Gathering information from multiple sources is useful in understanding children's skills across various settings. Families, for example, have a perspective on their children's skills from experiences at home that may differ from how teachers see children in a group, classroom setting.

What should happen to children who are *not ready* for school?

The NEGP concept of a ready school suggests that it is a school's responsibility to educate all children who walk through its door, regardless of whether children are ready or not ready. The idea of schools' readiness for children is also evident in state policies regarding school entry. Most states use age, not skill level, as the criterion for determining when a child is eligible—and legally entitled—to attend public school (Saluja, Scott-Little, & Clifford 2000). Thus a child's readiness should not be a factor in determining eligibility for kindergarten. However, practice does not always follow this philosophy. Some families, school administrators, and teachers may want to delay school entry based on children's readiness. But research suggests that delaying school entry does not generally benefit children. (See Marshall 2003 and Stipek 2002 for research summaries on the effects of delayed kindergarten entry.)

If a child is deemed not ready for school, preschool teachers and administrators can talk to the family and kindergarten teacher about the particular needs of the child and work together to develop strategies for improving the child's skills. If concerned that the child's skills are far behind those of her peers, the team may refer the child for screening to determine whether she has a disability. Recognizing

> **Multiple conversations will most likely be needed to enable a community to reach consensus about school readiness.**

> **Research suggests that delaying school entry does not generally benefit children.**

that school readiness concerns more than just the child, the team can also identify strategies all can use to support the child's success. The preschool teacher and administrator, for example, can discuss strategies for ensuring that the child receives high-quality, individualized, and developmentally appropriate instruction that addresses all five domains of development.

If the team believes that the child is considered not ready because of inappropriate expectations from school staff, then a larger effort is likely needed to bring about change. The next section of this article discusses these larger efforts to develop consensus on school readiness.

What if preschool and kindergarten programs differ in their expectations of readiness? How can they work together to set appropriate expectations?

Even with the work of the NEGP and multiple years of research and discussion, a common definition of school readiness remains elusive (Meisels 1999). Parents, preschool teachers, and kindergarten teachers—even within the same community—may differ in their expectations of school readiness (Graue 1993; NEGP 1993). Discussions about people's views of school readiness are needed to develop a community-wide set of expectations regarding school readiness.

Communities, schools, or preschool programs can sponsor school readiness forums in which families, teachers, administrators, and community leaders discuss school readiness. Individual preschool programs can host meetings to discuss school readiness among preschool teachers and parents from their program along with kindergarten teachers in their neighborhood schools. Multiple conversations most likely will be needed to enable the group to reach a consensus about school readiness.

Joint professional development and kindergarten transition activities can be helpful in minimizing differences in expectations between preschool and kindergarten programs (Firlik 2003). Public schools and early care and education programs in the school district could cosponsor staff training for preschool and kindergarten teachers. Such experiences may help teachers from different systems develop more views in common on readiness. Preschool teachers visiting kindergarten classrooms gain a better understanding of the kindergarten experiences their students will encounter. And when kindergarten teachers visit preschool classrooms, they appreciate and understand the preschool experiences their students have had.

What can I do to support appropriate practices regarding school readiness assessments?

Although the many challenges in ensuring that school readiness assessments are done appropriately require the efforts of many, every individual can make a difference. Here are some ways an individual can work to support the appropriate use of school readiness assessments.

Be informed. Reading about school readiness and participating in other professional development activities will help you develop expertise in this area.

> **Families . . . have a perspective on their children's skills from experiences at home that may differ from how teachers see children in a group, classroom setting.**

Get involved. Apply your expertise to the discussion of school readiness at the local, state, or national level. You can speak out to help ensure that school readiness assessment efforts benefit, not harm, young children. Start with your own program, making sure that you are using the appropriate instruments and procedures for your particular purpose and that the program's assessment results are used to help children.

Build partnerships. People have different perspectives about school readiness and school readiness assessments, which can lead to some heated discussions. Strengthening relationships with preschool teachers, administrators, families, and public school staff makes it easier to work together toward a common understanding of this controversial topic. If you work in an early care and education setting, reach out to kindergar-

> **When kindergarten teachers visit preschool classrooms, they appreciate and understand the preschool experiences their students have had.**

ten teachers to discuss your views of school readiness and assessment. If you are a kindergarten teacher, work with preschool teachers on school readiness issues.

References

AERA, APA, & NCME (American Educational Research Association, American Psychological Association, & National Council on Measurement in Education) Joint Committee on Standards for Educational and Psychological Testing. 1999. *Standards for educational and psychological testing*. Washington, DC: AERA.

Firlik, R. 2003. Early years summit: Preschool-kindergarten collaboration makes a difference. *Young Children* 58 (1): 73–78.

Gilliam, W., & E. Zigler. 2001. A critical meta-analysis of all evaluations of state-funded preschool from 1977 to 1998: Implications for policy, service delivery and program evaluation. *Early Childhood Research Quarterly* 15: 551–73.

Graue, M.E. 1993. *Ready for what? Constructing meanings of readiness for kindergarten*. Albany: State University of New York Press.

Kagan, S.L., E. Moore, & S. Bredekamp, eds. 1995. *Reconsidering children's early development and learning: Toward common views and vocabulary*. Washington, DC: National Education Goals Panel. Online: www.negp.gov/Reports/child-ea.htm

Lee, V.E., & D. Burkam. 2002. *Inequality at the starting gate: Social background differences in achievement as children begin school*. Washington, DC: Economic Policy Institute.

Love, J.M., J.L. Aber, & J. Brooks-Gunn. 1994. *Strategies for assessing community progress toward achieving the first national educational goal*. Princeton, NJ: Mathematica Policy Research.

Marshall, H. 2003. Research in Review. Opportunity deferred or opportunity taken? An updated look at delaying kindergarten entry. *Young Children* 58 (5): 84–93.

Maxwell, K.L., D.M. Bryant, S.M. Ridley, & L. Keyes-Elstein. 2001. *North Carolina's kindergartners and schools: Summary report*. Chapel Hill: University of North Carolina, Frank Porter Graham Child Development Center. Online: www.ncsmartstart.org/overview/facts/nckindersumm.pdf

Meisels, S. 1999. Assessing readiness. In *The transition to kindergarten*, eds. R.C. Pianta & M.J. Cox, 39–66. Baltimore, MD: Brookes.

NASBE (National Association of State Boards of Education). 1991. *Caring communities: Supporting young children and families*. Alexandria, VA: Author. Executive summary online: www.nasbe.org/educational_issues/reports/sum_caring_com.pdf.

NEGP (National Education Goals Panel). 1993. *The national education goals report. Volume one: The national report*. Washington, DC: U.S. Government Printing Office.

NEGP (National Education Goals Panel). 1997. *Getting a good start in school*. Washington, DC: U.S. Government Printing Office. Online: www.negp.gov/reports/good-sta.htm.

Niemeyer, J., & C. Scott-Little. 2001. *Assessing kindergarten children: A compendium of assessment instruments*. Tallahassee, FL: SERVE. Online: www.serve.org/publications/rdakcc.pdf.

North Carolina Ready for School Goal Team. 2000. *School readiness in North Carolina: Strategies for defining, measuring, and promoting success for all children*. Greensboro, NC: SERVE. Online: www.fpg.unc.edu/~SchoolReadiness/SRFullReport.pdf.

Saluja, G., C. Scott-Little, & R.M. Clifford. 2000. Readiness for school: A survey of state policies and definitions. *Early Childhood Research and Practice* 2 (2). Online: http://ecrp.uiuc.edu/v2n2/saluja.html.

Scott-Little, C., S.L. Kagan, & R.M. Clifford. 2003. *Assessing the state of state assessments: Perspectives on assessing young children*. Greensboro, NC: SERVE.

Shepard, L., S.L. Kagan, & E. Wurtz. 1998. *Principles and recommendations for early childhood assessments*. Washington, DC: National Education Goals Panel. Online: www.negp.gov/reports/prinrec.pdf.

Shore, R. 1998. *Ready schools: A report of the Goal 1 Ready Schools Resource Group*. Washington, DC: National Education Goals Panel. Online: www.negp.gov/reports/readysch.pdf.

Stipek, D. 2002. At what age should children enter kindergarten? A question for policy makers and parents. *Society for Research in Child Development Social Policy Report* 16 (2): 3–16. Online: www.srcd.org/sprv16n2.pdf.

West, J., K. Denton, & E. Germino-Hausken. 2000. *America's kindergartners: Findings from the Early Childhood Longitudinal Study, Kindergarten Class of 1998–99, fall 1998*. Washington, DC: U.S. Department of Education, National Center for Education Statistics.

Zill, N., & J. West. 2001. *Entering kindergarten: A portrait of American children when they begin school. Findings from the Condition of Education 2000*. NCES #2001-035. Washington, DC: U.S. Department of Education, National Center for Education Statistics. Online: http://nces.ed.gov/pubs2001/2001035.pdf.

NAEYC Position Statements Related to School Readiness

NAEYC assists policy makers and other stakeholders in their decision making through the adoption and dissemination of position statements. NAEYC's position on school readiness was adopted by the NAEYC Governing Board in July 1990 and revised in 1995 (www.naeyc.org/positionstatements/school_readiness).

In this position statement NAEYC affirms that a commitment to promoting universal school readiness requires resources and other supports to ensure that all children have access to the experiences that promote school success; recognition of individual differences among children, such as differences in skills, home languages, families' values and beliefs, and so on; and appropriate expectations for children as they enter school, based on an understanding of typical child growth and development.

Other NAEYC position statements that address school readiness issues include the following:

• Early Childhood Curriculum, Assessment, and Program Evaluation: Building an Effective, Accountable System in Programs for Children Birth through Age 8 (joint position with the National Association of Early Childhood Specialists in State Departments of Education [NAECS/SDE]): www.naeyc.org/positionstatements/cape

• Early Learning Standards: Creating the Conditions for Success (joint position with NAECS/SDE): www.naeyc.org/positionstatements/learning_standards

• STILL Unacceptable Trends in Kindergarten Entry and Placement (NAECS/SDE position, endorsed by NAEYC): www.naeyc.org/positionstatements/psunacc.pdf

• Learning to Read and Write: Developmentally Appropriate Practices for Young Children (joint position with the International Reading Association): www.naeyc.org/positionstatements/learn_readwrite

• Early Childhood Mathematics: Promoting Good Beginnings (joint position with the National Council of Teachers of Mathematics): www.naeyc.org/positionstatements/mathematics

Ensuring Culturally and Linguistically Appropriate Assessment of Young Children

Rosa Milagros Santos

Ensuring implementation of appropriate assessment procedures continues to be a struggle for early childhood researchers and practitioners. The negative ramifications for young children and their families of inappropriate assessment and testing procedures are well documented, particularly for those of diverse cultural and linguistic backgrounds (Donovan & Cross 2002). In most cases such inappropriate actions lead to misdiagnosis of learning needs and the mis- and overidentification of children for placement in special education programs (Donovan & Cross 2002).

Assessment problems often stem from a lack of training, awareness, and sensitivity on the part of the professionals who plan and conduct the procedures. Lack of awareness and sensitivity can inadvertently lead to the selection and use of assessment materials and tools that do not take into account variations in children's skills and knowledge based on cultural and linguistic differences. For example, some language assessment tools ask the child to identify items that are unique to the primary U.S. culture, such as a picture of Raggedy Ann. A child unfamiliar with this toy may not be able to respond correctly, which may bias his or her score and misrepresent the child's abilities.

Researchers suggest that professionals need to deepen their understanding of the impact of culture and language on the assessment process (Donovan & Cross 2002; McLean 2004). Several available resources can help professionals develop their knowledge of culturally and linguistically appropriate assessments. One source is the Early Childhood Research Institute on Culturally and Linguistically Appropriate Services (CLAS).

CLAS offers valuable Internet-based resource materials designed to assist professionals, family members, policy makers, and others in ensuring that assessments are culturally and linguistically appropriate. The goals of the CLAS Institute are "to identify, evaluate, and promote effective and appropriate early intervention practices and preschool practices that are sensitive and respectful to children and families from culturally and linguistically diverse backgrounds" (Fowler, Santos, & Corso 2004). Its Web site (http://clas.uiuc.edu) offers an easy-to-navigate search option for materials that can be individualized to one's needs.

CLAS's Web site includes information on more than four thousand materials collected from across the United States on various topics related to early childhood, including assessment. Many materials have been reviewed for cultural and linguistic appropriateness. Recommendations by CLAS reviewers regarding the appropriateness of many of the materials help potential users make informed decisions before they purchase or use these materials in their communities.

One useful tool accessible through the CLAS Web site is the set of review guidelines for individuals or early childhood teams to use in reflecting upon and discussing the cultural and

© Jonathan A. Meyers

Rosa Milagros Santos, PhD, is an assistant professor in the Department of Special Education at the University of Illinois at Urbana-Champaign. Her research focuses on the influence of culture and language on services for young children and their families.

linguistic appropriateness of specific materials. CLAS describes the guidelines as "developed through a collaborative effort of a diverse group of individuals from across the country, representing a variety of disciplines, cultures, races, languages, and ethnicity" and as "based on the current knowledge base in the fields of early childhood special education, early intervention, early childhood education, special education, medicine, and humanities" (Fowler, Santos, & Corso 2004).

CLAS guidelines can be helpful to teams as they develop materials or decide whether or not to purchase or use materials. Review guidelines related to assessment include reflective statements and questions focusing on the overall quality of the material and practices around assessment planning, conducting assessments, and analyzing and reporting assessment results. Considerations in selecting culturally and linguistically appropriate assessment materials and tools are included. A total of 17 review guidelines are available online or can be ordered; a sampling is given here in "Some Considerations for Appropriate Assessment."

Review guidelines on other assessment-related topics are found on the CLAS Web site. Screening and family information gathering resources are also available.

Great strides have been made to ensure the appropriate assessment of young children and their families, but still larger challenges lie ahead. Recognizing the impact of culture and language on the assessment process is a first step. It starts us in a direction that assures children's access to a promising future.

> **Professionals need to deepen their understanding of the impact of culture and language on the assessment process.**

References

Donovan, M.S., & C.T. Cross, eds. 2002. *Minority students in special and gifted education.* Division of Behavioral and Social Sciences and Education, Committee on Minority Representation in Special Education, National Research Council. Washington, DC: National Academies Press.

Fowler, S.A., R.M. Santos, & R.M. Corso, eds. 2004. *CLAS collection #1: Getting started: Culturally and linguistically appropriate screening, assessment, and family information gathering.* Longmont, CO: Sopris West.

McLean, M. 2004. Conducting child assessments. In *CLAS collection #1: Getting started: Culturally and linguistically appropriate screening, assessment, and family information gathering,* eds. S.A. Fowler, R.M. Santos, & R.M. Corso. Longmont, CO: Sopris West.

Some Considerations for Appropriate Assessment

Planning the assessment. Seek each family's view on native language maintenance and the learning of another language. Honor families' preferred language or mode of communication by (1) having persons fluent in that language conduct the assessment or (2) reviewing the assessment tool to identify if it is sensitive to or mismatched with cultural norms or language usage.

Choosing materials. Make sure the language in the material acknowledges diversity (e.g., family structures, multigenerations, disabilities, gender, ethnicity, socioeconomic status, religion, and so on). Check the design, illustrations, and photos to determine whether they represent a nonstereotypical view of cultural and linguistic groups (e.g., contemporary dress).

Conducting the assessment. Assessment includes determining eligibility, services, and monitoring procedures. Professionals should seek assistance from a family member or cultural guide to confirm their interpretations of the child's behavior during the assessment process.

Analyzing and reporting. Results can be in written or oral format. Include a qualified representative of the child's cultural and linguistic group to assist in the interpretation of the results when bilingual professionals are not available. Have the assessment team consider to what degree perceived developmental delays are related to cultural or childrearing practices, difficulties in translation, or other factors.

In 1990 NAEYC and the National Association of Early Childhood Specialists in State Departments of Education (NAECS/SDE) published a joint position statement on early childhood curriculum and assessment. Since that time, significant trends and contemporary issues, research findings, and new understandings of and changes in practice have influenced early childhood education. Many changes have had positive effects, but other changes are less positive, raising concerns about how they may affect children's development, learning, and access to services. Under the guidance of a committee of NAEYC Governing Board members, NAECS/SDE leaders, and other experts, the position statement has been substantially revised to address critical issues and to reflect new knowledge about curriculum, assessment, and program evaluation as they affect children from birth through age eight.

These pages offer a very brief description of where we stand (www.naeyc.org/positionstatements/cape) on these issues, with the position statement's key recommendations and indicators of effectiveness. The full position statement "Early Childhood Curriculum, Assessment, and Program Evaluation: Building an Effective, Accountable System in Programs for Children Birth through Age 8" may be downloaded from NAEYC's Web site (www.naeyc.org/positionstatements/cape). The position statement with expanded resources is also available online. These resources include

- a discussion of trends and issues;
- presentation of guiding principles and values;
- evidence-based rationales for each recommendation, with extensive references;
- a "Frequently Asked Questions" section to further explain and clarify each recommendation; and
- developmental charts that provide examples of how each recommendation may be implemented in programs for infants and toddlers, preschoolers, kindergartners, and primary grade children.

Where We Stand

On Curriculum, Assessment, and Program Evaluation

NAEYC and NAECS/SDE

What should children be taught in the years from birth through age eight? How would we know if they are developing well and learning what we want them to learn? And how could we decide whether programs for children from infancy through the primary grades are doing a good job?

Answers to these questions—questions about *early childhood curriculum, child assessment,* and *program evaluation*—are the foundation of a joint position statement from NAEYC and the National Association of Early Childhood Specialists in State Departments of Education (NAECS/SDE).

The position statement's recommendations

Curriculum

Implement curriculum that is thoughtfully planned, challenging, engaging, developmentally appropriate, culturally and linguistically responsive, comprehensive, and likely to promote positive outcomes for all young children.

Indicators of effective curriculum

- Children are active and engaged.
- Goals are clear and shared by all.
- Curriculum is evidence based.
- Valued content is learned through investigation, play, and focused, intentional teaching.
- Curriculum builds on prior learning and experiences.
- Curriculum is comprehensive.
- Professional standards validate the curriculum's subject matter content.
- The curriculum is likely to benefit children.

Assessment

Make ethical, appropriate, valid and reliable assessment a central part of all early childhood programs. To assess young children's strengths, progress, and needs, use assessment methods that are developmentally appropriate, culturally and linguistically responsive, tied to children's daily activities, supported by professional development, inclusive of families, and connected to specific, beneficial

---

Position Statement Revisions Committee

Lindy Buch and Maurice Sykes, *Cochairs* • Susan Andersen • Elena Bodrova • Jerlean Daniel • Linda Espinosa • Dominic Gullo • Marlene Henriques • Jacqueline Jones • Mary Louise Jones • Deborah Leong • Ann Levy • Christina Lopez Morgan • Joyce Staples • Marilou Hyson and Peter Pizzolongo, *NAEYC staff*

purposes: (1) making sound decisions about teaching and learning, (2) identifying significant concerns that may require focused intervention for individual children, and (3) helping programs improve their educational and developmental interventions.

Indicators of effective assessment practices

- Ethical principles guide assessment practices.
- Assessment instruments are used for their intended purposes.
- Assessments are appropriate for ages and other characteristics of children being assessed.
- Assessment instruments are in compliance with professional criteria for quality.
- What is assessed is developmentally and educationally significant.
- Assessment evidence is used to understand and improve learning.
- Assessment evidence is gathered from realistic settings and situations that reflect children's actual performance.
- Assessments use multiple sources of evidence gathered over time.
- Screening is always linked to follow-up.
- Use of individually administered, norm-referenced tests is limited.
- Staff and families are knowledgeable about assessment.

Program evaluation and accountability

Regularly evaluate early childhood programs in light of program goals, using varied, appropriate, conceptually and technically sound evidence to determine the extent to which programs meet the expected standards of quality and to examine intended as well as unintended results.

Indicators of effective program evaluation and accountability

- Evaluation is used for continuous improvement.
- Goals become guides for evaluation.
- Comprehensive goals are used.
- Evaluations use valid designs.
- Multiple sources of data are available.
- Sampling is used when assessing individual children as part of large-scale program evaluation.
- Safeguards are in place if standardized tests are used as part of evaluations.
- Children's gains over time are emphasized.
- Well-trained individuals conduct evaluations.
- Evaluation results are publicly shared.

Creating change through support for programs

Implementing the preceding recommendations for curriculum, child assessment, and program evaluation requires a solid foundation. Calls for better results and greater accountability from programs for children in preschool, kindergarten, and the primary grades have not been backed up by essential supports for teacher recruitment and compensation, professional preparation and ongoing professional development, and other ingredients of quality early education.

The overarching need is to create an *integrated, well-financed system of early care and education* that has the capacity to support learning and development in all children, including children living in poverty, children whose home language is not English, and children with disabilities. Unlike many other countries, the United States continues to have a fragmented system for educating children from birth through age eight, under multiple auspices, with greatly varying levels of support, and with inadequate communication and collaboration.

Many challenges face efforts to provide all young children with high-quality curriculum, assessment, and evaluation of early childhood programs. *Public commitment,* along with *investments* in a well-financed system of early childhood education and in other components of services for young children and their families, will make it possible to implement these recommendations fully and effectively.

Beyond Curriculum, Assessment, and Program Evaluation: What Else Matters?

Without other essential components of high-quality early childhood education, these recommendations will be of limited value. Learn more about

- **early learning standards,** as described in NAEYC and NAECS/SDE's 2002 position statement, online at www.naeyc.org/positionstatements/learning_standards.

- **teaching strategies** and other elements of developmentally appropriate practice. See *Developmentally Appropriate Practice in Early Childhood Programs Serving Children from Birth through Age 8,* 3d ed., eds. C. Copple & S. Bredekamp (Washington, DC: NAEYC, 2009). The position statement is online at www.naeyc.org/positionstatements/dap.

- **standards for early childhood programs** and accreditation performance criteria, online at www.naeyc.org/positionstatements.

- **standards for professional preparation** of early childhood educators. See *Preparing Early Childhood Professionals: NAEYC's Standards for Programs,* ed. M. Hyson (Washington, DC: NAEYC, 2003). This document is online at www.naeyc.org/positionstatements/ppp.

The Words We Use

A Glossary of Terms for Early Childhood Education Standards and Assessments

Jana Martella

The Early Childhood Education Assessment Consortium (ECEA) online glossary had its roots in the 2002 NAEYC Professional Development Leadership Institute. Participants gathered to discuss the draft joint position statement on standards being developed by NAEYC and the National Association of Early Childhood Specialists in State Departments of Education (NAECS/SDE). (See www.naeyc.org/resources/position_statements/creating_conditions.asp.) Several participants noted that even the simplest words related to standards and assessments for young children are burdened with unclear meanings or different meanings, depending on who is considering them.

An informal group of enthusiastic "lexicographers" agreed to take on the ambitious task of developing a glossary of key words related to standards and assessment for young children. They hoped to provide clarity for the field by creating a consensus listing of the most essential and relevant words and then linking the definitions of these words to resources for delving deeper into their meanings.

Over the next several months, the dictionary developers winnowed down the list of terms to be defined, divided the labor, and fine-tuned a framework for the task. The focus would be on early learning standards and assessments with a broad view of development. They expected that the resulting glossary would be dynamic, timely, and easily changed or updated, and therefore best suited to a Web-based format.

Throughout their deliberations, the lexicographers pursued and scrutinized well-researched definitions. The resulting lexicon, "The Words We Use: A Glossary of Terms for Early Childhood Education Standards and Assessments," became a reality. It defines 31 primary terms. Each primary word is followed by a group of important related terms that enlarge its meaning and provide a scaffold of additional information. In many cases the related terms are also defined and linked.

Web and print links tie each primary term to other academic and research-based definitions. These delineate the seminal sources from which the meaning was derived and allow the reader to explore the term in greater depth and compare the analysis in the glossary with those of other experts.

The lexicographers decided that the glossary would not contain test measurement and statistical terms that have widely accepted meanings, such as *valid, reliable, norm,* and *standard score.* Likewise the glossary does not provide information on specific test instruments. However, comprehensive sources for this information are provided

Jana Martella, MS, is the director of early childhood and family education for the Council of Chief State School Officers (CCSSO) in Washington, D.C. She has 25 years of experience in education as a primary teacher and assistant administrator, legislative liaison, and state coordinator for federal programs. A central part of her work focuses on education system and program improvement through standards-based reform, including promoting improved opportunities in early childhood education.

within the introduction, and the Web sites noted earlier will take the user to more technical information.

The glossary is designed as an online resource. The Web format permits it to be expanded to include additional words that would benefit from definitions specific to use with young children, and it allows for changes in meaning that may occur over time. Readers can expect to find new words added to the glossary on a regular basis and can suggest additional words online.

The lion's share of credit for development of the glossary goes to Harriet Egertson, early childhood specialist for the Nebraska Department of Education at the beginning of the project. Later, as an independent consultant, she provided leadership, coordination, expertise, and guidance, in addition to writing many of the definitions. Particular thanks are also owed to Susan Andersen, early childhood consultant in the Iowa Department of Education. Her energy as coordinator of the Council of Chief State School Officers' (CCSSO) Early Childhood Education Assessment State Collaborative on Assessment (ECEA-SCASS) helped initiate the effort. Appreciation goes to Dianne Rothenberg, codirector of the Early Childhood and Parenting Collaborative Information Technology Group; her energy and passion for words and their meanings contributed to the framework for the endeavor. The other members of the Lexicon team (p. 44) contributed significantly to early drafts and throughout the review process.

> For additional information about ECEA-SCASS, see www.ccsso.org/projects/SCASS/Projects/Early_Childhood_Education_Assessment_Consortium/ or contact Jana Martella, CCSSO's director of early childhood and family education, at janam@ccsso.org.

Glossary of Terms

accommodations: Adaptations in assessment tools and standards to permit children with disabilities or English-language learners to show what they know and can do. Adjustments may be made, for example, in the way a test is administered or presented, in the timing, in the language, or in how the child responds. The nature of the adjustment determines whether or not what is being measured or the comparability of scores is affected.

accountability: An organization's or individual's responsibility for developing and implementing a process or procedure to justify decisions made and to demonstrate the results or outcomes produced (e.g., what progress children are making).

achievement test: A testing instrument, typically standardized and norm referenced, used to measure how much a child has learned in relation to educational objectives.

alternative assessment: The terms *alternate assessment* and *alternative assessment* are also used to describe accommodations made to enable children with disabilities to participate in the assessment process. See *performance-based assessment* and *accommodation*.

aptitude test: A testing instrument intended to predict a child's ability to do or learn something, given an opportunity to learn.

assessment: A systematic procedure for obtaining information from observation, interviews, portfolios, projects, tests, and other sources that can be used to make judgments about characteristics of children or programs.

authentic assessment: See *performance-based assessment*.

benchmarks (performance standards): Clear, specific descriptions of knowledge or skill that can be supported through observations, descriptions and documentations of a child's performance or behavior and by samples of the child's work; often used as points of reference in connection with more broadly stated content standards.

content standards: Statements that provide a clear description of what a child should know and be able to do in a content area at a particular level.

criterion-referenced test: A testing instrument in which the test taker's performance (i.e., score) is interpreted by comparing it with a prespecified standard or specific content and/or skills.

developmental assessment: An ongoing process of observing a child's current competencies (including knowledge, skills, dispositions, and attitudes) and using the information to help the child develop further in the context of family and caregiving and learning environments.

documentation: Documentation is the process of keeping track of and preserving children's work as evidence of their progress or of a program's development.

early learning standards: Statements that describe expectations for the learning and development of young children across the domains of health and physical well-being; social and emotional well-being; approaches to learning; language development and symbol systems; and general knowledge about the world around them.

evaluation: The measurement, comparison, and judgment of the value, quality, or worth of children's work and/or of their schools, teachers, or a specific educational program, based upon valid evidence gathered through assessment.

formal assessment: A procedure for obtaining information that can be used to make judgments about characteristics of children or programs using standardized instruments.

indicators: Various statistical values, data, or other reported information that, when aggregated, provides an indication of the condition or direction of movement relative to a standard or issue under study.

informal assessment: A procedure for obtaining information that can be used to make judgments about characteristics of children or programs using means other than standardized instruments.

ASSESSMENT 43

Glossary of Terms (continued)

norm-referenced test: A standardized testing instrument by which the test taker's performance is interpreted in relation to the performance of a group of peers who have previously taken the same test. The group of peers is known as the norming group.

observational assessment: A process in which the teacher systematically observes and records information about the child's level of development and/or knowledge, skills, and attitudes in order to make a determination about what has been learned, improve teaching, and support children's progress. A checklist or notes are often used to record what has been observed.

outcomes: Changes in behavior, knowledge, understanding, ability, skills, and/or attitudes that occur as a result of participation in a program or course of study, receiving services, or using a product.

performance standards: See *benchmarks*.

performance-based (alternate, alternative, authentic) assessment: Any assessment strategy designed to estimate a child's knowledge, understanding, ability, skill, and/or attitudes in a consistent fashion across individuals emphasizing methods other than standardized achievement tests, particularly those using multiple choice formats. Performance-based assessments typically include exhibitions, investigations, demonstrations, written or oral responses, journals, and portfolios.

portfolio assessment: A collection of work, usually drawn from children's classroom work, which, when subjected to objective analysis, becomes an assessment tool. This occurs when (1) the assessment purpose is defined; (2) criteria or methods are made clear for determining what is put into the portfolio, by whom, and when; and (3) criteria for assessing either the collection or individual pieces of work are identified and used to make judgments about children's learning.

program standards: Widely accepted expectations for the characteristics or quality of early childhood settings in homes, centers, and schools. Such characteristics typically include the ratio of adults to children; the qualifications and stability of the staff; characteristics of adult-child relationships; the program philosophy and curriculum model; the nature of relationships with families; the quality and quantity of equipment and materials; the quality and quantity of space per child; and safety and health provisions.

readiness test: A testing instrument designed to measure skills believed to be related to school learning tasks and to be predictive of school success.

rubrics: Descriptive scales for organizing and interpreting data gathered from observations of children's performance on a learning task and/or of children's developmental status. Rubrics describe levels of performance of children's work or a particular area of knowledge by defining varying levels of quality or mastery and providing indicators of each level.

screening: The use of a brief procedure or instrument designed to identify, from within a large population of children, those who may need further assessment to verify developmental and/or health risks.

standardized test: A testing instrument that is administered, scored, and interpreted in a standard manner. It may be either norm referenced or criterion referenced.

standards: Widely accepted statements of expectations for children's learning or the quality of schools and other programs.

standards-based assessment: A process through which the criteria for assessment are derived directly from content and/or performance standards.

test: One or more questions, problems, and/or tasks designed to estimate a child's knowledge, understanding, ability, skill, and/or attitudes in a consistent fashion across individuals. Information from a test or tests contributes to judgments made as a part of an assessment process.

The Lexicon Team

Susan R. Andersen
Early Childhood Consultant, Iowa Department of Education

Elena Bodrova
Senior Researcher, Mid-continent Research for Education and Learning (McREL)

Karen C. Curtis
Doctoral Student, George Mason University/NAEYC Intern

Harriet A. Egertson
Independent Consultant

Marilou Hyson
Associate Executive Director for Professional Development, NAEYC

Sharon Lynn Kagan
Professor, Teachers College, Columbia University

Debora Leong
Professor, Metropolitan State College of Denver

Jana Martella
Director, Early Childhood and Family Education, Council of Chief State School Officers

Oralie McAfee
Professor Emeritus, Metropolitan State College of Denver

Oralia Puente
Senior Project Associate, Council of Chief State School Officers

Dianne Rothenberg
Codirector, Early Childhood and Parenting Collaborative Information Technology Group, University of Illinois at Urbana-Champaign

Catherine Scott-Little
Project Director, Regional Educational Laboratory at SERVE

Ann Segal
President, Action Strategies

The Words We Use: A Glossary of Terms for Early Childhood Education Standards and Assessments is online at www.ccsso.org/eceaglossary.

Assessing Children's Development
Strategies That Complement Testing

Ann S. Epstein, Lawrence J. Schweinhart, and Andrea DeBruin-Parecki

Early childhood practitioners assess young children's learning and development to let themselves, families, administrators, and policy makers know how the children are doing and to learn how much a program or setting has contributed to that. Sometimes people think traditional testing—a series of multiple-choice questions, for example—is the only way to assess children's learning and development. But that is far from the case. Such testing has an important but limited role, focusing only on those areas of children's learning and development that have right answers, such as simple facts and arithmetic. It focuses on the answers individual children provide on their own rather than through collaborative problem solving. It focuses on the answers children give at a specific period of time and in a specific physical and social setting.

Other forms of child assessment complement traditional testing by providing additional important information about children's learning—such as how they use what they know to solve real-life problems in everyday settings. They include objective observations, portfolio analyses of individual and collaborative work, and teacher and parent ratings of children's behavior. These methods involve richer, more varied interaction between adults and children, are more open ended, and often look at performance over an extended period of time.

An example of a particular type of objective observation, High/Scope's new Early Literacy Assessment (ELA) (DeBruin-Parecki 2004) evaluates the early literacy skills of young children three to five years old by having an adult read to a child a specially developed storybook. The storybook contains assessment questions focused on the four key principles of early literacy: alphabetic principle, phonological awareness, concepts about print, and comprehension. The ELA is administered in a familiar context

© Ellen B. Senisi

Ann S. Epstein, PhD, is early childhood director of the High/Scope Educational Research Foundation. She has developed early childhood curriculum, training, and assessment materials and conducted research at High/Scope since 1975.

Lawrence J. Schweinhart, PhD, is president of High/Scope. He has conducted research on early childhood programs since 1975, particularly the High/Scope Perry Preschool Study and the validation of the High/Scope Preschool Child Observation Record, and served as research chair from 1989 to 2003.

Andrea DeBruin-Parecki, PhD, is director of High/Scope's Early Childhood Reading Institute. She has developed authentic assessments in the areas of early and family literacy and has been actively involved in literacy research focusing on populations at high risk for academic failure.

> It is important to know which tests and what conditions of administration will guarantee that we **do no harm** to children and that we **acquire valid information.**

and environment and does not rely on unrealistic time constraints, enabling children to be comfortable responding. In these circumstances, it is likely that young children will be better able to demonstrate what they know and understand.

Concern about assessment in the early childhood field is not new. Decades of debate are summarized in NAEYC's publication *Reaching Potentials: Appropriate Curriculum and Assessment for Young Children* (Bredekamp & Rosegrant 1992) and its joint position statement "Early Childhood Curriculum, Assessment, and Program Evaluation: Building an Effective, Accountable System in Programs for Children Birth through Age 8" (NAEYC & NAECS/SDE 2003). What is new is the heightened attention to testing young children as a means of holding programs accountable for their learning. Why is heightened attention to appropriate child assessment a timely conversation? Because states are developing prekindergarten assessments and school readiness assessments, and the nation's largest assessment of four- and five-year-olds, the Head Start National Reporting System (NRS) test (Head Start Bureau 2003), may become established in Head Start policy as well as a model beyond Head Start programs.

Several prominent early childhood assessment experts have criticized the Head Start NRS regarding reliability and validity, cultural and linguistic appropriateness, testing of every child versus sampling, and use of the data. As of spring 2004, the test involved only literacy and mathematics; the other areas of the Head Start Outcomes Framework were not considered in this controversial test. It is important for Head Start programs to assess children's development and be held accountable for the quality of programs and services. Hopefully, in the future the Head Start Bureau will move carefully toward identifying the assessment tools and procedures that will serve its young children and their teachers well.

It appears that the rationale for this testing policy is included in the No Child Left Behind Act and supported by the report of the National Reading Panel (NICHD 2000). The assumption is that young children should acquire a prescribed body of knowledge and academic skills to be ready for school. Social aspects of school readiness, while also touted as essential in a series of National Research Council reports (notably *Eager to Learn* [Bowman, Donovan, & Burns 2000] and *From Neurons to Neighborhoods* [Shonkoff & Phillips 2000]), are neither as widely mandated nor as measurable by typical tests as their academic counterparts. Social and emotional skills do not figure as prominently in the testing and accountability debate.

Given the pervasive use of testing, it is important to be clear about its proper role in a comprehensive assessment system and under what conditions traditional testing can be used appropriately with preschool-age children. It is important to know which tests and what conditions of administration will guarantee that we do no harm to children and that we acquire valid information. Given that even well-designed tests can provide only one type of datum, we must also consider how to use the various types of assessments that combine to give a full and balanced picture of children's development. Traditional tests do serve an important purpose, but they do not help teachers and families engaged in the day-to-day support of children's learning.

Photos © Karen Philips

Other ways to assess children's development

Various kinds of assessments complement traditional tests. They are sometimes called *authentic assessments* because they engage children in tasks that are personally meaningful, take place in real-life contexts, and are grounded in naturally occurring learning activities. These assessment methods offer multiple options to evaluate motivation, achievement, and attitudes, as well as children's learning of right answers. They provide information that can be used to guide teaching and enhance learning.

Authentic assessments are consistent with the curriculum goals and instructional practices of the program in which they are used (Paris & Ayres 1994). They rely on realistic time frames and allow children plenty of time to show evidence of what they know and can apply in everyday settings. Progress toward mastery is the key, and content is mastered as a means, not as an end (Wiggins 1992). For example, it is important to measure whether children can use their knowledge of numbers to solve everyday problems (how many napkins to give out at snack time), not merely to recite digits aloud by rote. To document accomplishments, assessments must note the starting point (baseline) and the end point (outcome) and be sensitive to incremental changes along the way.

Like traditional tests, authentic measures must meet psychometric standards of reliability and validity. Their use, especially on a widespread scale, requires adequate resources. Assessors must be trained to acceptable levels of reliability. Data collection, coding, entry, and analysis can take a lot of time and cost a lot of money. This investment is reasonable and necessary, however, to yield valid information. Other child assessment procedures that can meet the criteria of reliability and validity include observations, portfolios, and ratings of children by teachers and parents. These are described, along with examples, in the sections that follow.

> **L**ike traditional tests, authentic measures must meet psychometric **standards of reliability and validity. Their use, especially on a widespread scale, requires** adequate resources.

> **A**necdotal notes should serve as the raw data for completing validated developmental scales **that define categories of behaviors rather than single right answers.**

Systematic observation and documentation

Systematic observation and documentation of children's activities in their day-to-day settings doesn't require that children be removed from the program setting, nor does it pose unnatural or unfamiliar demands on their attention or actions. Although careful observation requires effort, the approach intrudes minimally into what childrn are doing and has high ecological validity—that is, it represents well the actual settings in which such behavior typically takes place. Moreover, observation is a comprehensive form of assessment since children's activities normally integrate all dimensions of their development—intellectual, motivational, social-emotional, physical, and aesthetic. (See "Observations, Documentation, and Planning," p. 48)

Anecdotal notes alone, however, are not sufficient for good assessment. They need to be judged against criteria for children's progress and provide a basis for collecting evidence of reliability and validity. Anecdotal notes should serve as the raw data for completing validated developmental scales that define categories of behaviors rather than single right answers. For example, the Work Sampling System (Meisels et al. 2001) employs developmental checklists with statements such as "Shows comfort and confidence with self" followed by the response alternatives "not yet," "in process," and "proficient." Rated anecdotal notes allow and expect teachers to set the framework for children to initiate their own activities. This method embraces a broad definition of child development that includes not only literacy and mathematics, but also initiative, social relations, physical skills, and the arts. It is culturally sensitive because trained observers—be they teachers or outside data collectors—focus on objective, culturally neutral descriptions of behavior ("Pat hit Bob") rather than subjective, culturally loaded interpretations ("Pat was very angry with Bob"). Finally, observational methods empower teachers by recognizing their judgment as essential to accurate assessment.

Observations, Documentation, and Planning

Observations provide information that helps teachers assess behavior and knowledge, systematically plan instructional activities, and meet curriculum standards. Here is an example of how observations permit documentation and planning in the development of early mathematics skills (adapted from Graves 2000).

There was a circular structure around the base of a large oak in the school yard that preschoolers called the tree house. As the weather warmed and the snow melted, children began to notice how the tree house was changing. Teachers recorded the following observations over a week:

> Peter and Keisha collected fallen pieces of splintering bark and sorted them into three piles they labeled "babies" (small), "mommies" (medium), and "daddies" (large). Elizabeth came over and counted the chips in each pile, restacking them as she counted each number aloud. "This one's kinda big," she said. "Can I put it in the daddy pile?" Keisha said okay.
>
> Juan climbed on the tree house and touched the second branch above his head. "Look, I can reach higher now. That's because I'm almost five."
>
> Emma stood on the side of the tree house that doesn't get much sun. "The wood is darker here. It's still wet."
>
> Ibrahim whispered to Eli, "Let's hide under the tree house so Megan [the teacher] can't find us." When they emerged, Eli said, "I found an acorn. It fell down from the tree when it rained."

The teachers scored these and other anecdotes using the Preschool Child Observation Record (COR) (High/Scope 2003), a validated and widely used measure using five-point scales for documenting different areas of development. They noted that individual children showed the following developmental levels on the COR mathematics and science items:

Sorting attributes, level 4: In sorting, child groups objects that are the same in some way and identifies the similarities *(Peter and Keisha)*

Identifying patterns, level 3: Child arranges 3 or more objects in a graduated series *(Peter, Keisha, and Elizabeth)*

Comparing properties, level 4: Child uses a comparison word to describe the difference between two objects *(Juan and Emma)*

Counting, level 2: Child counts objects, naming one number for each object *(Elizabeth)*

Identifying position and direction, level 2: Child uses a position word *(Ibrahim and Eli)*

Identifying natural and living things, level 1: Child names a natural object or material *(Eli)*

Capitalizing on the renewed interest in the tree house, the teachers planned a painting experience to provide more opportunities for making comparisons. They set out the following materials: paint brushes of different widths; blue, red, and white paint; different size containers for mixing paints; and water for washing up. Here are some of their observations from this planned activity:

> Emma said she was going to paint three boards pink. When Jack [another teacher] wondered how much paint she would need, Emma pointed to a medium-size bucket and said, "I'm going to put red and white paint all the way to the top."
>
> Ibrahim painted four boards and described his work, saying, "Red, blue, red, blue."
>
> Juan announced, "Painting is hard work. Hey, you guys, use the thick brush. It's faster."

Children's spontaneous activities and the intentional experiences planned by teachers enabled these preschoolers to participate in key experiences related to classification (e.g., exploring and describing similarities, differences, and the attributes of things); seriation (e.g., arranging several things in a series or pattern); number (e.g., counting objects); space (e.g., experiencing and describing positions, directions, and distances in the play space); and time (e.g., experiencing and describing rates of movement) (Hohmann & Weikart 2002). The activities also encompassed the standards of the National Council of Teachers of Mathematics (NCTM 2000): number (e.g., count with understanding and recognize how many in sets of objects); algebra (e.g., sort, classify, and order objects by size, number, and other properties); geometry (e.g., compare and sort two- and three-dimensional shapes); measurement (e.g., recognize the attributes of length, volume, weight, area, and time); and data (e.g., pose questions and gather data about themselves and their surroundings).

Portfolios

One of the most fitting ways to undertake meaningful student assessment is through the use of a well-constructed portfolio system. A portfolio is "a purposeful collection of student work that tells the story of the student's efforts, progress, or achievement in (a) given area(s). This collection must include student participation in selection of portfolio content, the guidelines for selection, the criteria for judging merit, and evidence of student self-reflection" (Arter & Spandel 1992, 36). Portfolios describe the process of a child's learning as well as the final product. They provide rich information and involve multiple sources of data collected over a representative period of time. (See "Portfolios in Preschool.")

Portfolios have additional value. They encourage collaboration between children, teachers, and families; promote ownership and motivation; integrate assessment with instruction and learning; and establish a quantitative and qualitative record of progress.

Courtesy of the authors

Portfolios in Preschool

Courtesy of the authors

Portfolios allow teachers to track individual growth over time in different areas of development. In the following illustrations, Benjamin's progression in visual art is documented with two dated portfolio entries. Because he wanted to take the actual work home, his teacher took photographs of Benjamin's work (and Benjamin at work) to include in his portfolio.

At small group time, the teacher provided pieces of wood, a large jar of paste with a pump handle, and a paper cup for each child. Children pumped as much paste as they wanted into their cups, and assembled and attached the wooden pieces to create sculptures. Benjamin began by randomly stacking and pasting two blocks and one dowel on a flat base, but he was more interested in exploring the properties of the paste than creating a finished product.

At small group time three months later, the teacher provided children with paper, scissors, and hole punches. Benjamin carefully cut a diagonal off one corner of the paper, chose a butterfly-shaped hole punch, and systematically made holes around the perimeter of the paper until he returned to the starting point. When he was finished, he announced, "I made a butterfly airport."

Benjamin stayed with each task for a long time. His concentration was evident in his facial expression. In notes accompanying the portfolio entries, Benjamin's teacher annotated his work according to the developmental progressions documented in the Arts Education Partnership standards for visual arts in early childhood (AEP 1998).

From accidental to intentional representation: In the first work, Benjamin is interested in exploring materials, not making something concrete or recognizable. In the second work, he accidentally creates a form and only then decides it looks like something (a butterfly airport). In the future, Benjamin can be expected to intentionally create an object or event with representative materials he chooses ahead of time.

From simple to elaborated models: In the first work, Benjamin focuses on the overall sensory experience rather than specific details. In the second entry, he focuses on two details—cutting the corner to his specifications and working his way all around the rim with the hole punch. Over time, Benjamin will be able to hold more than two visual attributes in mind.

From marks and lines to shapes and figures: In the first work, motion and manipulation are ends in themselves. The pleasure of a repetitive action is also evident in Benjamin's use of the hole punch. However, he has also advanced to the second stage, where lines and textures are controlled. In a later stage, Benjamin will deliberately produce shapes and figures.

From random marks to relationships: At first, Benjamin's marks and shapes are unrelated to one another. The production of each is a self-contained experience. In his second work, the marks bear a deliberate relationship to one another and to the composition as a whole. The marks are evenly spread (equidistant) around the paper's edge, and Benjamin systematically rotates the paper as he reaches each corner. His intention is to cover the entire rim.

Benjamin's teacher shared these notations with his family to help them understand and appreciate the developmental significance of their son's artistic explorations. Annotating portfolios with developmental stages also alerted the teacher to where her students were and where they could be expected to go in the coming months. The teacher was thus able to provide a variety of materials and tools that encouraged each child to explore and progress at his or her own developmental pace.

ASSESSMENT

"Portfolios encourage teachers and students to focus on important student outcomes, provide parents and the community with credible evidence of student achievement, and inform policy and practice at every level of the educational system" (Herman & Winters 1994, 48).

Portfolios are most commonly used for assessment in elementary and secondary schools. Yet they have long been used in preschools to document and share children's progress with families, administrators, and others. For program accountability, as well as children's learning and reflection, the evaluated outcomes must be aligned with curriculum and instruction. Children must have some choice about what to include in order to feel ownership and pride. Portfolios should document the creative process as well as the product, encouraging children to reflect on their actions. Conversations with children about their portfolios further engage their desire to demonstrate their increasing knowledge and skills. Sharing portfolios with parents can help teachers connect school activities to the home and involve parents in their children's education.

Teacher and parent ratings

Ratings are another way to organize teacher perceptions of children's development into scales for which reliability and validity can be assessed. In contrast to observations of specific and detailed behavior, ratings tend to assess more general student characteristics. Children's grades on report cards are the most common type of teacher rating system. They are generally

> **P**ortfolios should document the creative *process as well as the product, encouraging children to reflect on their actions.*

Teacher Ratings as Assessment

Teacher ratings are a relatively simple and inexpensive form of assessment. This makes them an attractive supplement to (and occasionally substitute for) other measures. However, teacher ratings can be useful only if they yield accurate information. Here is an example of a statewide study that shows teachers are a knowledgeable and trustworthy source of student data.

In evaluating the Michigan School Readiness Program (MSRP) for four-year-olds at risk for school failure, the High/Scope Educational Research Foundation used various types of assessments (Xiang et al. 2000). The evaluation compared 338 children who participated in MSRP with 258 children of similar age and socioeconomic background who did not participate. All were followed from their entrance into kindergarten through fourth grade.

Among the assessment measures was a series of scales that asked elementary school teachers to rate children in their classes on a variety of academic and social dimensions. Teachers did not know whether the children they were rating had been in MSRP or were part of the comparison group. Children who had been in the program were found to be significantly more ready for school than those who had not participated. The teacher ratings indicated that MSRP children

- were more interested in school
- had better attendance
- took more initiative
- retained learning better
- were stronger in reading, mathematics, and thinking skills
- were better problem solvers
- worked better with others

Teacher ratings were validated by demonstrating significant relationships with other measures, including the Michigan Educational Assessment Program (MEAP), a statewide test of academic achievement. More MSRP children than comparison children passed the MEAP literacy and mathematics sections. Teacher ratings also correlated significantly with observational data collected with the Child Observation Record (COR) (High/Scope 2003). Children who completed the state-funded preschool program were significantly more advanced than the other children in key areas of development—language and literacy, creative representation, music and movement, initiative, and social relations.

These findings show that when teacher ratings are used to assess objectively defined academic and social behavior, they can provide valid data to follow children's progress and track program accountability.

derived from students' performance on indicators with objective scoring procedures, such as examinations or projects evaluated according to explicitly defined criteria. For example, to complete the Devereux Early Childhood Assessment (see www.devereuxearly childhood.org/monograph.html) for a child, the teacher and parent each rate the frequency (*never, rarely, occasionally, frequently,* or *very frequently*) of a particular behavior (e.g., shares with other children). In these ways, teacher ratings can be specifically related to other types of child assessments, including scores on multiple-choice tests or other validated assessment tools, concrete and specific behavioral descriptions (e.g., frequency of

Photos © Karen Phillips

participation in group activities, ability to recognize the letters in one's name), or global assessments of children's traits (e.g., cooperative, sociable, hard-working). Research shows that teacher ratings can have considerable short- and long-term predictive validity throughout later school years and even into adulthood (Schweinhart, Barnes, & Weikart 1993). (See "Teacher Ratings as Assessment.")

Parent ratings, like teacher ratings, can organize adult perceptions of children's development into scales for which reliability and validity can be assessed. Soliciting parent ratings is an excellent way for teachers to involve them as partners in the assessment of their children's performance. The very process of completing scales can inform parents about the kinds of behaviors and milestones that are important in young children's development. It also encourages families to observe and listen to their children as they gather the data

> **The very process of completing scales can inform parents about the kinds of behaviors and milestones that are important in young children's development.**

needed to rate their children's performance. In this way, parent ratings—like all good assessment tools—serve an educational or training function as well as a data-gathering role. (See "Parent-Teacher Collaboration in Assessment," pp. 52–53)

The importance of parents, not only as child rearers but also as consumers of child care and preschool services for young children, is reflected in the increased use of parent ratings as a research and evaluation tool. For example, in the large-scale and comprehensive Head Start Family and Child Experiences Survey (FACES) study, parents' ratings of their children's abilities and progress were related to measures of classroom quality and child outcomes (Zill et al. 2003).

Conclusion

Recent years have seen growing public interest in early childhood education. Along with that support has come the use of assessment to justify the expense and use of the dollars. With so much at stake—the future of our nation's children—it is imperative that we proceed correctly. Above all, we must guarantee that assessment reflects our highest educational goals for young children and neither restricts nor distorts the substance of their early learning. A comprehensive and balanced assessment system meets the need for accountability while respecting the welfare and development of young children. Appropriate assessment helps teachers and families support children's positive learning outcomes. Such a system can include testing that measures applicable knowledge and skills in a safe and child-affirming situation. It should also include other forms of assessment that meet psychometric standards of reliability and validity.

Developing and implementing a balanced, child-friendly approach to assessment is not an easy or inexpensive undertaking. However, if we want a clearer

> **We must guarantee that assessment reflects our highest educational goals for young children and neither restricts nor distorts the substance of their early learning.**

picture of what young children actually know and understand and how educators can best support that learning, it is an investment worth making.

References

AEP (Arts Education Partnership). 1998. *Young children and the arts: Making creative connections—A report of the Task Force on Children's Learning and the Arts: Birth to age eight.* Washington, DC: Author.

Arter, J.A., & V. Spandel. 1992. NCME [National Council on Education in Measurement] instructional model: Using portfolios of student work in instruction and assessment. *Educational Measurement: Issues and Practice* 11 (1): 36–44.

Banks, N. 2001. Involving parents in curriculum planning: A Head Start story. In *Supporting young learners: Ideas for child care providers and teachers, volume 3,* ed. N.A. Brickman, 333–40. Ypsilanti, MI: High/Scope Press.

Bowman, B., M.S. Donovan, & M.S. Burns, eds. 2000. *Eager to learn: Educating our preschoolers.* A report of the National Research Council. Washington, DC: National Academies Press.

Bredekamp, S., & T. Rosegrant, eds. 1992. *Reaching potentials: Appropriate curriculum and assessment for young children, volume 1.* Washington, DC: NAEYC.

DeBruin-Parecki, A. 2004. *Early Literacy Assessment.* Ypsilanti, MI: High/Scope Press.

Graves, M. 2000. Young children and math. *High/Scope Extensions* 15 (2): 1–3.

Head Start Bureau, Administration on Children, Youth and Families, Administration for Children and Families, U.S. Department or Health and Human Services. 2003, June 26. *Information memorandum: Implementation of the Head Start National Reporting System on Child Outcomes.* Log no. ACYF-IM-HS-03-07. Online: www.headstartinfo.org/publications/im03/im03_07.htm.

Herman, J.L., & L. Winters. 1994. Portfolio research: A slim collection. *Educational Leadership* 52 (2): 48–55.

High/Scope Educational Research Foundation. 2003. *Preschool Child Observation Record.* 2nd ed. Ypsilanti, MI: High/Scope Press.

Hohmann, M., & D.P. Weikart. 2002. *Educating young children: Active learning practices for preschool and child care programs.* 2nd ed. Ypsilanti, MI: High/Scope Press.

HSB (Head Start Bureau). 2002. *Head Start Program Performance Standards and other regulations.* Washington, DC: U.S. Government Printing Office. Online: www.acf.hhs.gov/programs/hsb/performance.

Meisels, S.J., J. Jablon, D.B. Marsden, M.L. Dichtelmiller, A.B. Dorfman. 2001. *The Work Sampling System.* 4th ed. Ann Arbor, MI: Rebus. Online: www.pearsonearlylearning.com/index2.html.

NAEYC & NAECS/SDE (National Association of Early Childhood Specialists in State Departments of Education). 2003. Early childhood curriculum, assessment, and program evaluation: Building an effective, accountable system in programs for children birth through age 8. Online: www.naeyc.org/positionstatements/cape.

NCTM (National Council of Teachers of Mathematics). 2000. *Principles and standards for school mathematics.* Reston, VA: Author. Online: http://standards.nctm.org.

NICHD (National Institute of Child Health and Human Development). 2000. *Report of the National Reading Panel. Teaching children to read: An evidence-based assessment of the scientific research literature on reading and its implications.* (NIH Publication No. 00-4769). Washington, DC: U.S. Government Printing Office.

Paris, S.G., & L.R. Ayers. 1994. *Becoming reflective students and teachers with portfolios and authentic assessment.* Washington, DC: American Psychological Association.

Schweinhart, L.J., H.V. Barnes, & D.P. Weikart. 1993. *Significant benefits: The High/Scope Perry Preschool Study through age 27.* Ypsilanti, MI: High/Scope Press.

Shonkoff, J.P., & D.A. Phillips, eds. 2000. *From neurons to neighborhoods: The science of early childhood development.* A report of the National Research Council. Washington, DC: National Academies Press.

Wiggins, G. 1992. Creating tests worth taking. *Educational Leadership* 49 (8): 26–33.

Xiang, Z., L. Schweinhart, C. Hohmann, C. Smith, & E. Storer. 2000. *Points of light: Third year report of the Michigan School Readiness Evaluation.* Ypsilanti, MI: High/Scope Educational Research Foundation.

Zill, N., L. Resnick, K. Kwang, K. O'Donnell, & A. Sarongon. 2003. *Head Start FACES 2000: A whole child perspective on program performance: Fourth progress report.* Washington, DC: Administration for Children and Families, U.S. Department of Health and Human Services.

Parent-Teacher

The Head Start Program Performance Standards (HSB 2002) (online at www.acf.hhs.gov/programs/hsb/performance) state that "parents must be invited to become integrally involved in the development of the program's curriculum and educational approach...provided opportunities to increase child observation skills to share assessments with staff... [and] encouraged to participate in staff-parent conferences and home visits and discuss their child's development and education" (Part 1304.21a2). A Head Start program in rural Mississippi wanted to meet this standard with a meaningful yet doable option. Because the program used the High/Scope approach, the teachers focused on familiarizing parents with the curriculum's key experiences for child development and soliciting their help in collecting anecdotes to score the Preschool Child Observation Record (COR) (High/Scope 2003). They invited parents to become involved in anecdotal note taking and team planning for their child, either in person in the classroom (as parents' schedules permitted) or from home via telephone, e-mail, or other forms of home-school communication. Here is how the process worked for three-year-old Atien (adapted from Banks 2001).

Collaboration in Assessment

At the beginning of the school year, Atien's teacher (Cora) and her mother (Mae) set goals for Atien. Their main focus was in the COR category Initiative. Like many young three-year-olds, Atien was not yet following routines consistently. She moved rapidly from one interest area to another without focusing on one play idea for any length of time. Mae's work schedule did not allow her to come in for meetings, so she telephoned the school during her coffee breaks and sent in notes she had taken at home. Mae's notes informed Cora about Atien's current play interests:

Atien went around the house today smelling everything. She said, "This smells like apples!" (I was baking apple pie.) "This smells like daddy!" (She'd climbed on the dresser and sprayed his aftershave on her hand.) Atien also played in water several times this week. Last night she refused to get out of the tub. She helped me rinse dishes and wanted to rinse them again when we were done. On two days, she ran water in the bathroom sink and washed all her dolls.

Cora sent home an activity sheet she derived from COR that listed opportunities for Atien to participate in home routines. For example, under the suggestion to create a daily schedule using your child's interests as clues for each part of the routine, Cora wrote, "For Atien, the clues might be smells such as orange peel for breakfast, detergent for washing dishes after dinner, and toothpaste for bedtime."

To encourage Atien's active participation in the classroom, Cora used what Mae had written about her interest in water play and smells. She made sure the house area sink had water, set up a water table as a bath station for dolls, added fruit-scented playdough in the art area, and planned a small group activity in which the children would guess what was in "smelly jars" and write their ideas on poster board. Atien held up the list as children reviewed the accuracy of their guesses. At mealtime, Cora encouraged children to sniff the air and guess what would be served. During large group, Cora introduced songs, finger plays, and stories about water and smells.

At conference time, Mae and Cora compared notes. Atien had not only participated in school routines, but she had also reminded teachers when it was mealtime ("I can smell it") and pointed out the accuracy of her smelly-jar guesses. She'd given detailed plans for work time ("I'll use the cherry playdough and make two pies for Mommy") and had organized a complex play sequence for washing dolls that included a bathing area, a drying area, and a dressing area, each with accompanying materials. When a cup proved insufficient for filling the basin with water, she'd gotten a bucket from the art area.

At home, Atien had helped set the table and wash dishes. She'd talked animatedly and in great detail about the smells of the food and the sequence of steps in after-dinner cleanup. Bedtime was easier because Atien looked forward to taking a bath and reading a book she'd written with her mother about a little girl who plays at the lake all day.

Using these anecdotes, Mae and Cora completed the following Initiative items on the COR:

Making choices and plans, level 4: Child makes a plan with one or two details.

Initiating play, level 3: Child engages in pretend play.

Solving problems with materials, level 4: Child tries two ways to solve a problem with materials.

Taking care of personal needs, level 4: Child identifies the need for a tool and uses it independently to accomplish a personal goal.

Following the conference, Mae set new goals for Atien, focusing on Social Relations, another COR category. She said she would take notes on Atien's interactions with family and friends at home, while Cora said she would document interchanges with teachers and peers at school. They would continue to share notes and score another set of developmental scales at the next meeting.

Mae also reflected on the amount of time she'd spent assessing her daughter. She estimated it took 15 minutes at the end of each day to record anecdotal notes, plus 15 minutes for each of two telephone conferences. She concluded that the insights she'd gained into her daughter's development, plus her ability to contribute to the teacher's classroom plans, were well worth this reasonable investment of time. Mae added, "Atien enjoyed my paying attention to her and writing things down. It helped me see more of the good things she was doing."

Choosing an Appropriate Assessment System

Amy Lynn Shillady

How should early childhood educators select an appropriate assessment tool? First, it is important to understand what a developmentally appropriate, valid, reliable, and ethical assessment looks like. Some background research can provide this information. The joint position statement from NAEYC and the National Association of Early Childhood Specialists in State Departments of Education, "Early Childhood Curriculum, Assessment, and Program Evaluation," with expanded resources (NAEYC & NAECS/SDE 2003), includes recommendations and indicators of effectiveness, frequently asked questions, and other resources that can serve as guides in the selection of assessment tools (online at www.naeyc.org/positionstatements/cape).

The next step is to identify the age group for whom the assessment tool will be used (infant/toddler, preschool, etc.), the goals of the program, the purposes for which the assessment will be used, and other factors, such as children's cultures, languages, and abilities or disabilities.

The good news is that there is a wide variety of assessments to choose from, and a great deal of information about them is available online. There are numerous tools and systems designed to measure overall development, literacy, or social/emotional development.

A few of the many assessment options that are appropriate for preschool children are listed in the accompanying chart, which also describes important elements such as the adaptability of the assessment system and the preparation required. (These data are for informational purposes only. NAEYC does not endorse any of the assessment materials presented. Assessment tools and systems are developed for specific purposes and should not be used in ways that fall outside those designated guidelines.)

Amy Lynn Shillady, MA, is editor/publications manager at the National Child Care Information Center (NCCIC). She has worked with NAEYC's Professional Development department and NHSA's Research and Evaluation Department. A former Head Start teacher in Richmond, Virginia, Amy also has been a research consultant for Harvard University's Graduate School of Education.

References

Dickinson, D.K., A. McCabe, & K. Sprague. 2003. Teacher Rating of Oral Language and Literacy (TROLL): Individualizing early literacy instruction with a standards-based rating tool. *The Reading Teacher* 56 (6): 554–65.

Dodge, D.T., L. Colker, & C. Heroman. 2002. *The creative curriculum for early childhood.* 4th ed. Washington, DC: Teaching Strategies.

Early Childhood Research Institute on Measuring Growth and Development. 1998. *Technical report 4: Research and development of Individual Growth and Development Indicators for children between birth and age eight.* Minneapolis, MN: Author.

High/Scope Staff. 1992. *High/Scope Child Observation Record: For ages 2½-6.* Ypsilanti, MI: High/Scope Press.

LaFreniere, P.J., & J. E. Dumas. 1995. *Social Competence and Behavior Evaluation (SCBE): Preschool edition.* Los Angeles: Western Psychological Services.

LeBuffe, P.A., & J.A. Naglieri. 1998. *The Devereux Early Childhood Assessment (DECA).* Villanova, PA: Devereux Foundation.

Meisels, S., F. Liaw, A. Dorfman, & R.R. Nelson. 1995. The Work Sampling System: Reliability and validity of a performance assessment for young children. *Early Childhood Research Quarterly* 10 (3): 277–96.

NAEYC & NAECS/SDE (National Association of Early Childhood Specialists in State Departments of Education). 2003. Joint Position Statement. Early childhood curriculum, assessment, and program evaluation: Building an effective, accountable system in programs for children birth through age 8. Washington, DC: NAEYC. Online: www.naeyc.org/positionstatements/cape.

Assessment Tools for 3- to 5-year-olds

Assessment Tool	Assessment Domain(s)	Type of Assessment	Sample Items	Preparation
The Creative Curriculum Developmental Continuum (Dodge, Colker, & Heroman 2002) Spanish version available Teaching Strategies Inc. P.O. Box 42243 Washington, DC 20015 Phone: 800-637-3652 Fax: 202-364-7273 info@teachingstrategies.com www.teachingstrategies.com	Assesses social/emotional, physical, cognitive, and language development	Teacher Observational Rating Scale (Teachers observe and document children's learning, analyze observation notes, and use the Developmental Continuum to identify which step children have reached for each of the Creative Curriculum's 50 objectives)	Curriculum objective: Classifies objects (each step represents the developmental point in a sequence that children typically demonstrate as they progress toward mastering an objective) Forerunners: Finds two objects that are the same and comments or puts them together Step I: Sorts objects by one property, such as size, shape, color, or use Step II: Sorts a group of objects by one property and then by another *10/29—Sandra sorted leaves by size, then color.* Step III: Sorts objects into groups/subgroups and can state reason	Training is offered through national conferences, on-site workshops, technical assistance services. For more information about on-site training, phone 800-637-3652, ext. 22, or e-mail StaffDev@TeachingStrategies.com.
The Devereux Early Childhood Assessment (DECA) (LeBuffe & Naglieri 1998) Spanish version available The Devereux Foundation 444 Devereux Dr. Villanova, PA 19085 Phone: 610-542-3109 DECA@Devereux.org www.devereuxearlychildhood.org	Assesses social/emotional development (initiative, self-control, and attachment)	Teacher and Parent Observational Rating Scale (Teachers and families each complete the DECA for the child and review the results together.)	"During the past 4 weeks, how often did the child…" *Calm herself/himself down when upset?* "Place a check mark next to the word that tells how often you saw the behavior." ___ Never ___ Rarely ___ Occasionally ___ Frequently ___ Very frequently	DECA Program Training Options include basic implementation training, local program mentor training, and other training opportunities, such as "Classroom Strategies for Reducing Behavioral Concerns." For more training information, phone 866-TRAINUS or e-mail DECA@Devereux.org.

Note: Data are provided for informational purposes only. NAEYC does not endorse any of the assessment materials presented.

(Continued on p. 56)

ASSESSMENT

Assessment Tools for 3- to 5-year-olds (cont'd)

Assessment Tool	Assessment Domain(s)	Type of Assessment	Sample Items	Preparation
High/Scope Preschool Child Observational Record (COR) (High/Scope Staff 1992) Spanish version of Family Report Forms and Parent Guides included High/Scope Educational Research Foundation 600 N. River St. Ypsilanti, MI 48198-2898 Phone: 734-485-2000 Fax: 734-485-0704. info@highscope.org www.highscope.org	Assesses initiative, social relations, creative representation, movement and music, language and literacy, and mathematics and science	Teacher Observational Rating Scale (Teachers observe and document children's learning and analyze observation notes to identify which step children have reached for each objective)	Observational Item: Making Choices and Plans Level I: Child indicates a choice by pointing or some other action. *11/21—At circle time, Alem pointed to the game she wanted to play.* Level II: Child expresses a choice in one or two words. Level III: Child expresses a choice with a short sentence. Level IV: Child makes a plan with one or two details. Level V: Child makes a plan with three or more details.	Training options include one- and two-day workshops, week-long institutes, and multiple-week courses at High/Scope Foundation headquarters in Michigan or on site by request. For more training information, phone 734-485-2000, ext. 218, or e-mail training@highscope.org.
Social Competence and Behavior Evaluation (SCBE) (LaFreniere & Dumas 1995) Western Psychological Services (WPS) 12031 Wilshire Blvd. Los Angeles, CA 90025-1251 Phone: 800-648-8857 Fax: 310-478-7838 custsvc@wpspublish.com www.wpspublish.com	Assesses social/emotional development (social competence, emotional expression, and adjustment)	Teacher Observational Rating Scale	"Accepts compromises when reasons are given."	Training Manual provides observational, documentation, and scoring procedures.

Assessment Tool	Assessment Domain(s)	Type of Assessment	Sample Items	Preparation
Preschool Individual Growth and Development Indicators (IGDIs) (Early Childhood Research Institute on Measuring Growth and Development 1998) EC Research Institute on Measuring Growth & Development University of Minnesota 202 Pattee Hall 150 Pillsbury Dr., SE Minneapolis, MN 55455 Phone: 612-624-8020 Fax: 612-625-2093 pries005@umn.edu www.getgotgo.net	Assesses language and literacy skills (picture naming, alliteration, and rhyming)	Standardized Test administered by teachers on an individualized basis (using stimulus cards)	Sample Rhyming Stimulus Card: "Point to the one **[sweep finger across three pictures at bottom of card]** that rhymes or sounds the same as ____ **[point to and say the name of the top picture]**."	Background information, assessment instructions, stimulus materials, and data reporting resources can be downloaded at www.getgotgo.net.
Teacher Rating of Oral Language and Literacy (TROLL) (Dickinson, McCabe, & Sprague 2003) Center for the Improvement of Early Reading Achievement University of Michigan School of Ed., Rm. 2002 SEB 610 E. University Ave. Ann Arbor, MI 48109-1259 Phone: 734-647-6940 Fax: 734-615-4858 ciera@umich.edu www.ciera.org	Assesses literacy skills (language use, reading, and writing)	Teacher Observational Rating Scale (Teachers can rate competence in English and in child's native language)	"Does child recognize his or her own first name in print?" <u>No</u> <u>Yes</u> 1 2	Training Manual provides observational, documentation, and scoring procedures.
The Work Sampling System (Meisels et al. 1995) Pearson Early Learning Center P.O. Box 2500 Lebanon, IN 46052 Phone: 800-211-8378 Fax: 800-841-8939 customer_service@pearsonearlylearning.com www.pearsonearlylearning.com	Assesses personal and social development, language and literacy, mathematical thinking, scientific thinking, social studies, the arts, and physical development and health	Observational checklists, portfolios, and teacher and parent summary reports	Portfolio Core Item in the Scientific Domain: *Dante's collection of data on plant growth from 5/1 to 6/1*	To request on-site training or to learn more about Pearson Early Learning Center's Summer Institute training workshops, phone 888-832-9378 or 800-782-0801.

Print and Online Resources That Spotlight Young Children and ASSESSMENT

compiled by Marian Marion, Gayle Mindes, and contributing authors

Almy, M., & C. Genishi. 1979. *Ways of studying children*. Rev. ed. New York: Teachers College Press.

Andersen, S. 1998. The trouble with testing. *Young Children* 53 (4): 25–29.

Bagnato, S.J., J.T. Neisworth, & S.M. Munson. 1997. *Linking assessment and early intervention: An authentic curriculum-based approach*. Baltimore, MD: Brookes.

Barr, M., D.A. Craig, D. Fisette, & M.A. Syverson. 1999. *Assessing literacy with the Learning Record: A handbook for teachers, grades K–6*. Portsmouth, NH: Heinemann.

Beneke, S. 1998. *Rearview mirror: Reflections on a preschool car project*. Urbana-Champaign, IL: ERIC Clearinghouse on Elementary and Early Childhood Education. ERIC ED 424977.

Bondurant-Utz, J. 2002. *A practical guide to assessing infants and preschoolers with special needs*. Columbus: Merrill.

Bredekamp, S., & T. Rosegrant, eds. 1992. *Reaching potentials: Appropriate curriculum and assessment for young children*. Vol. 1. Washington, DC: NAEYC.

Bredekamp, S., & T. Rosegrant, eds. 1995. *Reaching potentials: Transforming early childhood curriculum and assessment*. Vol. 2. Washington, DC: NAEYC.

Clay, M. 1993. *An observation survey of early literacy achievement*. Portsmouth, NH: Heinemann.

Marian Marion, PhD, has taught young children and now teaches courses in child guidance and early childhood classroom management at the University of Wisconsin–Stout. She is the author of two early childhood textbooks, one on guidance and one on assessment.

Gayle Mindes, EdD, is a professor of education at DePaul University in Chicago and author of *Assessing Young Children*. She is a project evaluator for the Chicago Teacher Collaborative: A Project to Establish a Unit for Personnel Training, School Practice, and School Development in Special Education.

Cohen, D., V. Stern, & N. Balaban. 1996. *Observing and recording the behavior of young children*. New York: Teachers College Press.

Curtis, D., & M. Carter. 2000. *The art of awareness: How observation can transform your teaching*. St. Paul, MN: Redleaf.

Dale-Easley, S., & K. Mitchell. 2003. *Portfolios matter: What, where, when, why, and how to use them*. Markham, Ontario, Canada: Pembroke.

Dixon, S.D., K. Davis, & M.K. Schmidt. 1994. *Assessment in action: Ongoing observation in the classroom*. Bloomington, IN: Institute for the Study of Developmental Disabilities.

Dodge, D., L.J. Colker, & C. Heroman. 2002. *The Creative Curriculum Developmental Continuum Assessment System*. Washington, DC: Teaching Strategies.

Earl, L.M. 2003. *Assessment as learning: Using classroom assessment to maximize student learning*. Thousand Oaks, CA: Corwin.

Educational Testing Service. 2003. *Understanding standards-based assessment*. Pathwise series. Princeton, NJ: Author.

Espinosa, L.M. 2002. High-quality preschool: Why we need it and what it looks like. NIEER policy brief. *Preschool Policy Matters* no. 1: 1–11. Online: http://nieer.org/docs/index.php?DocID=58.

Freeman, N., & M. Brown. 2000. Evaluating the child care director: The collaborative professional assessment process. *Young Children* 55 (5): 20–28.

Genishi, C., ed. 1992. *Ways of assessing children and curriculum*. New York: Teachers College Press.

Grace, C., & E. Shores. 1998. *The portfolio book: A step-by-step guide for teachers*. Beltsville, MD: Gryphon House.

Gray, H. 2001. Initiation into documentation: A fishing trip with toddlers. *Young Children* 56 (6): 84–91.

Gronlund, G. 1998. Portfolios as an assessment tool: Is collection of work enough? *Young Children* 53 (3): 4–10.

Gullo, D.F. 1994. *Understanding assessment and evaluation in early childhood education*. New York: Teachers College Press.

Helm, J.H., & S. Beneke, eds. 2003. *The power of projects*. New York: Teachers College Press. Available from NAEYC.

Helm, J.H., S. Beneke, & K. Steinheimer. 1997. *Teacher materials for documenting young children's work: Using "Windows on Learning."* New York: Teachers College Press. Available from NAEYC.

Helm, J.H., S. Beneke, & K. Steinheimer. 1997. *Windows on Learning: Documenting young children's work*. New York: Teachers College Press. Available from NAEYC.

Hemmeter, M.L., K.L. Maxwell, M.J. Ault, & J.W. Schuster. 2001. *Assessment of practices in early elementary classrooms (APEEC)*. New York: Teachers College Press. Available from NAEYC.

Hill, B., & C. Ruptic. 1994. *Practical aspects of authentic assessment*. Norwood, MA: Christopher-Gordon Publishers.

Jablon, J.R., A.L. Dombro, & M.L. Dichtelmiller. 1999. *The power of observation*. Washington, DC: Teaching Strategies.

Jones, J. 2003. *Early literacy assessment systems: Essential elements*. Princeton, NJ: Policy Information Center, Educational Testing Service.

Jones, J., & R. Courtney. 2003. Documenting early science learning. In *Spotlight on young children and science*, eds. D. Koralek & L.J. Colker, 27–32. Washington, DC: NAEYC.

Katz, L.G. 1997. A developmental approach to assessment of young children. *ERIC Digest*. ERIC ED 407172.

Katz, L.G., & S.C. Chard. 1996. The contribution of documentation to the quality of early childhood education. *ERIC Digest*. ERIC ED 393608.

Katz, L.G., & S.C. Chard. 1997. Documentation: The Reggio Emilia approach. *Principal* 76 (5): 16–17.

Kohn, A. 2001. Fighting the tests: Turning the frustration into action. *Young Children* 56 (2): 19–24.

Krechevsky, M. 1998. *Project Spectrum. Preschool assessment handbook*. Vol. 3 in *Project Zero Frameworks for Early Childhood Education*, eds. H. Gardner, D.H. Feldman, & M. Krechevsky. New York: Teachers College Press.

Kuhs, T.M., R.L. Johnson, S.A. Agruso, & D.M. Monrad. 2001. *Put to the test: Tools and techniques for classroom assessment*. Portsmouth, NH: Heinemann.

Lazear, D. 1999. *Multiple intelligence approaches to assessment: Solving the assessment conundrum*. Rev. ed. Tucson: Zephyr.

Losardo, A., & A. Notari-Syverson. 2001. *Alternative approaches to assessing young children*. Baltimore: Brookes.

MacDonald, S. 1996. *The portfolio and its use: A roadmap for assessment (book 2)*. Little Rock, AR: Southern Early Childhood Association. Online: www.CreativeCurriculum.net.

Marsden, D.B., A.L. Dombro, & M.L. Dichtelmiller. 2003. *The Ounce Scale user's guide*. New York: Pearson Early Learning.

McAfee, O., & D. Leong. 2001. *Assessing and guiding young children's learning*. 3rd ed. New York: Pearson Allyn & Bacon.

Marshall, H. 2003. Research in Review. Opportunity deferred or opportunity taken? An updated look at delaying kindergarten entry. *Young Children* 58 (5): 84–93.

Meisels, S.J. 1995. Performance assessment in early childhood education: The Work Sampling System. *ERIC Digest*. ERIC ED 382407.

Meisels, S. 1999. Assessing readiness. In *The transition to kindergarten,* eds. R.C. Pianta & M.J. Cox, 39–66. Baltimore, MD: Brookes.

Meisels, S. 2000. On the side of the child—Personal reflections on testing, teaching, and early childhood education. *Young Children* 55 (6): 16–19.

Meisels, S.J., with S. Atkins-Burnett. 1994. *Developmental screening in early childhood: A guide.* 4th ed. Washington, DC: NAEYC.

Meisels, S.J., A.L. Dombro, D.B. Marsden, D.R. Weston, & A.M. Jewkes. 2003. *The Ounce Scale.* New York: Pearson Early Learning.

Mindes, G. 2003. *Assessing young children.* 2nd ed. Upper Saddle River, NJ: Prentice Hall/Merrill.

NAEYC & National Association of Early Childhood Specialists in State Departments of Education. 2003. Executive Summary. Early learning standards: Creating the conditions for success. *Young Children* 58 (1): 69–70.

NAEYC & National Association of Early Childhood Specialists in State Departments of Education. 2003. Joint Position Statement. Early childhood curriculum, assessment, and program evaluation: Building an effective, accountable system in programs for children birth through age 8. Online: www.naeyc.org/positionstatements/cape.

Owocki, G., & Y.M. Goodman. 2002. *Kidwatching: Documenting children's literacy development.* Portsmouth, NH: Heinemann.

Popham, W.J. 2000. *Testing! Testing! What every parent should know about school tests.* Boston: Allyn & Bacon.

Popham, W.J. 2002. *Classroom assessment: What teachers need to know.* 3rd ed. Boston: Allyn & Bacon.

Project Zero. 2003. *Making teaching visible: Documenting individual and group learning as professional development.* Cambridge, MA: Author.

Project Zero & Reggio Children. 2001. *Making learning visible: Children as individual and group learners.* Reggio Emilia, Italy: Reggio Children. Available from NAEYC.

Puckett, M.B., & J. Black. 2000. *Authentic assessment of the young child.* 2nd ed. Columbus, OH: Merrill.

Rating early childhood environments. 2003. Special issue, *Early Developments* 7 (2).

Ridley, S., & R.A. McWilliam. 2001. Putting the child back into child care quality assessment. *Young Children* 56 (4): 92–93.

Saluja, G., C. Scott-Little, & R.M. Clifford. 2000. Readiness for school: A survey of state policies and definitions. *Early Childhood Research and Practice* 2 (2). Online: http://ecrp.uiuc.edu/v2n2/saluja.html.

Sandall, S., M.E. McLean, & B.J. Smith, eds. 2000. *DEC recommended practices in early intervention/early childhood special education.* Denver: Division for Early Childhood.

Schweinhart, L. 1993. Observing young children in action: The key to early childhood assessment. *Young Children* 48 (5): 29–33.

Shepard, L., S.L. Kagan, & E. Wurtz, eds. 1998. *Principles and recommendations for early childhood assessments.* Washington, DC: National Education Goals Panel. Online: www.negp.gov/reports/prinrec.pdf.

Shepard, L., S. Kagan, E. Wurtz. 1998. Public Policy Report. Goal 1 Early Childhood Assessments Resource Group recommendations. *Young Children* 53 (3): 52–54.

Shores, E., & C. Grace. 1998. *The portfolio book: A step-by-step guide for teachers.* Beltsville, MD: Gryphon House.

Spodek, B., & O. Saracho, eds. 1997. *Issues in early childhood educational assessment and evaluation.* New York: Teachers College Press.

Testing's effects on schools and districts. 2003. Special issue, *Harvard Education Letter* 19 (4).

Waterman, B.B. 1994. Assessing children for the presence of a disability. Special issue, *News Digest* 4 (1). Online: www.nichcy.org/newsdig.asp#nd23.

Wellhousen, K. 1994. Assessment of early childhood social development. *Dimensions of Early Childhood* 23 (1): 32–35.

Wesson, K.A. 2001. The "Volvo effect"—Questioning standardized tests. *Young Children* 56 (3): 16–18.

Wheatley, K. 2003. Viewpoint. Promoting the use of content standards: Recommendations for teacher educators. *Young Children* 58 (2): 96–102.

Wortham, S.C. 2000. *Assessment in early childhood education.* 3rd ed. Upper Saddle River, NJ: Pearson Education.

Online resources

American Academy of Child and Adolescent Psychiatry offers public information pamphlets related to mental health and links to a wide variety of additional Web sites. www.aacap.org

Association for Supervision and Curriculum Development (ASCD) contains links on assessment. www.ascd.org

Center for Performance Assessment provides examples of teaching plans and position papers. www.makingstandardswork.com

Center for the Study of Testing, Evaluation, and Educational Policy (CSTEEP) shares position papers and policy statements on assessment and evaluation. www.csteep.bc.edu

CLAS (Culturally and Linguistically Appropriate Services) Early Childhood Research Institute, representing diverse cultural and linguistic roots, collects and describes early childhood/early intervention resources for children with disabilities and their families and the service providers who work with them. http://clas.uiuc.edu

Council for Exceptional Children is a clearinghouse for information about children with disabilities. Publications that facilitate teaching are described. www.cec.sped.org

"Critical Issue: Assessing Young Children's Progress Appropriately" provides analysis of the problems unique to assessing young children as well as goals, options for action, differing opinions, and links to illustrative cases. www.ncrel.org/sdrs/areas/issues/students/earlycld/ea500.htm

CTB McGraw-Hill is a corporate site on standardized tests, with glossary and position papers and test descriptions. www.ctb.com

Early Childhood Education Assessment (ECEA) Consortium provides information and resources to help states develop assessment systems that are appropriate for all children. Information about publications on assessment and a glossary of terms are on this site. www.ccsso.org/projects/SCASS/Projects/Early_Childhood_Education_Assessment_Consortium

Educational Testing Service offers test descriptions, position papers, and research related to tests and testing. www.ets.org

KidSource Online, a parent-operated site, covers a broad spectrum of issues related to assessment, observation, and teaching. www.kidsource.com

LD Online has information on learning disabilities for teachers, parents, and other professionals. www.ldonline.org

National Center for Fair and Open Testing is an advocacy organization with position papers on tests and assessment, a newsletter, and other activities. www.fairtest.org

National Center for Research on Evaluation, Standards, and Student Testing (CRESST) publishes updates and a newsletter, and holds conferences on assessment and standards. www.cse.ucla.edu

National Education Goals Panel (NEGP)—Although this bipartisan, intergovernmental body has been dissolved, its site offers an Interactive Data Center and publications, reports on states and national progress toward improving the educational lives of children, and policy recommendations. www.negp.gov

National Institute for Early Education Research includes a state data bank with information on content standards for early education. www.nieer.org/states

National PTA offers hints for parents to promote school success as well as a resource guide on diversity and other current issues. A search for *assessment* turns up No Child Left Behind information and more. www.pta.org

Project Spectrum lists a number of relevant articles on assessment. http://pzweb.harvard.edu/Research/Spectrum.htm

Project Zero at Harvard University is a source for research and information about applied multiple intelligences. http://pzweb.harvard.edu

Zero to Three provides articles and information on assessment and intervention for infants and toddlers. www.zerotothree.org

Reflecting, Discussing, Exploring

Questions and Follow-Up Activities

Heather Biggar

The articles in *Spotlight on Young Children and Assessment* represent just a small sample of the many valuable resources for early childhood educators interested in the assessment of young children and its role in promoting development and learning. For students in early childhood professional preparation programs, for early childhood teachers taking part in training and other forms of professional development, and for individuals seeking to broaden their understanding of this important topic, we hope these articles and the accompanying professional development resources (pp. 58–59) will open doors to further exploration of appropriate and effective assessment.

To help you reflect on and apply insights from these articles, we have developed a series of questions and suggested follow-up activities. The series begins with an invitation to think about your own early experiences of being assessed. Specific questions and suggested activities related to each article follow. Finally, we help you pull things together with general questions about curriculum, teaching practices, resources, and next steps.

Heather Biggar, PhD, is a professional development specialist at NAEYC.

A. Recalling your own early experiences

1. What memories do you have of early experiences being tested or being assessed in other ways? How did you feel when you knew testing was coming up, and how did those feelings change over time? In retrospect, can you think of times you were probably being assessed without being aware of it?

2. Do you remember any repercussions, positive or negative, related to the results of assessments or testing? What feelings—anxiety, pride, shame, relief—do you associate with being tested or evaluated? Share your memories with other adults, including those of different generations and cultures. What similarities and differences do you find?

B. Expanding on each article

"Framing the Assessment Discussion"/*Jacqueline Jones*

Why does assessment, and being able to discuss it knowledgeably, matter? Jacqueline Jones, an early childhood assessment specialist, explains the importance of having evidence of children's progress to understanding both children's and program development. She provides key questions stakeholders can use to participate in dialogues about assessment at various educational levels.

1. "Rapid and episodic learning…is a hallmark of early childhood," writes Jones. Sharpen your observation skills by keeping a log of one child's changes in interest, mood, energy level, and behavior at various times of the day for a week. What did you learn about the child? How can you use this information in your practice?

2. Even as adults we may have negative feelings about tests and other kinds of assessments. What benefits does Jones describe that result from these activities? How have they helped children you know or a program with which you are involved? Can you think of other benefits of assessment?

3. Jones cites five assessment targets or types of knowledge that programs should assess. How do you currently assess each of these targets in your classroom or program? What barriers to assessing each target have you encountered? What solutions could you implement to overcome those barriers?

"Beyond Outcomes: How Ongoing Assessment Supports Children's Learning and Leads to Meaningful Curriculum"/Diane Trister Dodge, Cate Heroman, Julia Charles, and Jessica Maiorca

The authors emphasize the importance of linking assessment to goals and objectives of the classroom curriculum. They explain how to evaluate where children are in their learning, use that knowledge to help them get to the next level, and show colleagues, families, and policy makers evidence that children are developing knowledge and skills.

4. Review the goals and objectives of the curriculum in your program or the program with which you are most familiar. Do the assessment methods you use indicate whether you are meeting each goal and objective? How can you use this information to improve educational outcomes for each child? If there are goals not covered by your current assessments, what are some ways you could assess them?

5. The authors suggest prominently displaying curriculum goals and objectives in your classroom. Make a poster depicting the major goals or objectives of the curriculum you use or one you are studying. The poster can help keep teachers on track and family and visitors informed.

6. Sharing information with others is an essential purpose of the assessment process. Examine the language, format, tone, and frequency with which you communicate assessment results to others—staff, teachers, families, representatives of funding agencies. Are there ways you can improve on your reporting? How do you know your audiences understand and interpret your findings as you intend?

"Infant/Toddler Assessment"/Margo L. Dichtelmiller and Laura Ensler

There are challenges and important benefits associated with assessing infants and toddlers. The authors describe firsthand their experience with Ensler's Early Head Start program implementing an assessment specifically designed for use with infants and toddlers.

7. The article begins by describing some of the challenges of assessing infants and toddlers. Have you ever wanted more information about an infant or toddler but felt it would be impossible to complete an accurate assessment? What challenges did you encounter, and how did you meet them?

8. The article cites four important benefits of assessing infants and toddlers. Think about an infant or toddler you know or who is in your program, and describe how assessment of that child would be beneficial. What positive results can occur for the child, the family, the caregivers, and the program?

9. For what reasons do the authors recommend using a functional assessment instead of a task-based assessment for very young children? Do you agree with their recommendation? Why or why not?

10. Some teachers may be uncomfortable with a functional assessment like the Ounce Scale because they are used to tests with "right" or "wrong" responses. After reading this article, how would you respond to those concerns? How do you feel about the approach used and the areas measured by the Ounce Scale?

"From Policing to Participation: Overturning the Rules and Creating Amiable Classrooms"/Carol Anne Wien

Carol Anne Wien describes the changes made when teachers in three programs looked critically at rules and physical environments with an eye toward simplifying and following children's lead. The changes led to less teacher stress and more collaborative, joyful communities.

11. Wien notes that a crucial moment in changing practice occurs when teachers reexamine their images of and beliefs about children. Take a moment to think about and write out a list of your beliefs about children. Now focus on the way you (or a teacher you have observed) teach, supervise, and interact with children; write down a few key words that characterize those interactions. Does the teaching style match the beliefs about children's abilities and needs? What openings do you see for changes that better honor your values about children?

12. Rules are important for guiding children's well-being and respect for others and the environment; yet, as the author shows, they can become more of a hindrance than a help. With colleagues or other students, write down all of the explicit rules used in a classroom with which you are familiar. Now list all the unwritten rules that are understood and generally followed by the children. What surprises you about these lists? Try to reduce the number of rules by combining those that overlap and eliminating those that are unnecessary. What reactions to the new list do you predict from teachers and children?

13. What aspects of children's behavior or the classroom environment would you measure to determine the impact of changes to the rules, the physical environment, or the general emotional tone? For example, would you measure incidences of aggression? Noise level? Opportunities for children to practice their negotiating skills? Length of children's concentration spans? What outcomes would you most like to see as a result of those changes?

14. What aspects of your own or other teachers' behavior, attitudes, and experiences would you assess in relation to reducing restrictive rules or otherwise improving the environment? Would you measure teacher stress levels, amount of time spent watching the clock, incidences of following children's lead, amount of time spent conversing or interacting with children, or attitude toward work? What teacher or staff outcomes would you most like to see as a result of those changes?

"School Readiness Assessment"/*Kelly L. Maxwell and Richard M. Clifford*

The authors, both of whom are early childhood researchers and scientists, explain that most school readiness assessments focus on only one piece of the puzzle—the children—when school readiness actually involves a broad array of people as well as the schools and the communities.

15. The article identifies five domains of children's development and learning as important to school success, based on the National Education Goals Panel: physical, social and emotional, approaches to learning, language, and cognitive domains. Do you think assessing each of these domains is equally important to school readiness? Is there any aspect of development or learning that you would add to the list?

16. The authors provide some guidance on how to choose school readiness assessments. Discuss the guidance and key questions with colleagues or a teacher to see how your program (or a program you know well) might improve on its school readiness assessment plans. Select one step you will implement or could recommend for implementation.

17. What, for you, are the critical advantages and disadvantages of using naturalistic versus standardized, norm-referenced school readiness assessments? Is there an approach that you favor or are required to use? If so, what advantages can you foresee of more fully incorporating an additional approach? Practice using a new approach at the next appropriate opportunity and note your reactions.

18. The article cites some specific ways an individual can support the appropriate use of school readiness assessments. What are they, and which of these steps might you take?

"Ensuring Culturally and Linguistically Appropriate Assessment of Young Children"/*Rosa Milagros Santos*

Rosa Milagros Santos is an experienced researcher on how culture and language influence services for young children and their families. Here she discusses the importance of understanding how culture and language influence children's performance on assessments.

19. Santos provides an example of the Raggedy Ann doll as an artifact of "the primary U.S. culture" that children from other cultures may not be readily able to identify. On your own or with others, see how many such items you can list.

20. Talk with colleagues or fellow students with children who have moved to the United States from another country. What concerns do they have about their child's education? Describe the obstacles they have encountered in establishing a daily routine and interacting with Americans. Do they want their family—children and adults—to assimilate to the U.S. culture, to retain the ways of their country of origin, or both? Why? How do they meet this goal?

21. Santos provides the Web address for CLAS (Culturally and Linguistically Appropriate Services), a useful resource for ensuring that assessments are culturally and linguistically appropriate. Go to the CLAS Web site (http://clas.uiuc.edu) and explore. What strikes you as interesting or surprising about the site? What barriers to assessment of children from other cultures and language backgrounds does it reveal? What are the basic assumptions, and do you agree with them? Look for resources available through the site that will help you or teachers you know support the development and learning of a particular child.

"Where We Stand"/*NAEYC and the National Association of Early Childhood Specialists in State Departments of Education*

The article discusses three components of early childhood classrooms: curriculum, assessment, and program evaluation.

22. Why do you think the authors of the position statement discuss these three components together rather than individually? Draw a diagram with lines, arrows, and other creative marks to show how activities in your classroom (or a classroom you have observed) connect these components to each other.

"Assessing Children's Development: Strategies That Complement Testing"/*Ann S. Epstein, Lawrence J. Schweinhart, and Andrea DeBruin-Parecki*

The authors discuss three approaches to assessing young children that complement traditional tests: observation and documentation, portfolios, and teacher and parent rating scales. These are sometimes called authentic assessments.

23. Of the three approaches presented—observation, portfolios, and teacher or parent rating scales—select the one with which you are least familiar, and find out more about it. You can research the approach by going online, talking to colleagues, or reading articles about effective assessments using that approach.

24. In the descriptions of the tree house and painting activities, the authors provide examples of how to find and structure observation activities. Following these models, select a specific activity in which to observe a group of children, then create a new activity that will allow you to expand and refine your observations of those children. Use a recording measure (such as the COR) or defined standards to rate each child's levels of development.

25. If you do not currently use a portfolio system, select one child or a small subset of children for whom to begin creating portfolios for assessment purposes. Be sure to consult with other staff and family members to share your plan and collect their input. If you already use a portfolio system, consider ways to enhance it based on suggestions from the article, such as increasing children's input in the selection of work samples, enhancing your annotations, or using the portfolio to improve communication with families.

26. Good teacher and parent ratings of children's performance are validated by data from other measures. Is there information about the children in your classroom that you lack but could collect using rating scales? Consult with an administrator or other knowledgeable source about rating scales you might use.

C. Making connections

Consider the big picture

1. In your view, what are the three most important themes or key ideas that recur throughout this group of articles? Compare your nominations with those identified by other readers.

2. Again thinking of the entire group of articles, what are three key teacher behaviors that support appropriate assessment of young children?

3. Because this is a small selection of articles, some important ideas may have been left out or underrepresented. In your mind, what is missing in this discussion of assessment? For example, how assessment might look in other cultures; how assessment has changed in recent generations; appropriate accommodations for children with disabilities; current legislative activity that could affect assessment. Where can you learn more about these topics?

Examine curriculum goals and expected outcomes

4. Read *Early Childhood Curriculum, Assessment, and Program Evaluation: Building an Effective, Accountable System in Programs for Children Birth through Age 8*, a joint position statement of NAEYC and the National Association of Early Childhood Specialists in State Departments of Education (NAECS/SDE) (online at www.naeyc.org/positionstatements). Although its key points are summarized in this book (pp. 51–53), the full position statement provides detailed recommendations and resources. Examine the recommendations, and discuss them in a group, or consider choosing one or more recommendations to present to colleagues or other students.

5. How does the choice of a curriculum and its implementation relate to choice and implementation of assessment, and vice versa? Consider how curriculum and assessment are interrelated, and how they relate to overarching program goals. What recommendations and indicators from the position statement (see question 4 above) are the same or similar for curriculum and assessment, and why might that be the case?

6. Imagine that you are neither required nor permitted to assess any of the children in your classroom. What difficulties and frustrations might you face? What questions would you be unable to answer? How would this affect your daily practice? Which aspects of conducting assessments, either in the process or in the results, would you miss?

Use reflection to enhance teaching practices

7. As you read and discuss this entire set of articles, what do you find that affirms your current practices? What questions do the articles raise about your practices? What new approaches might you try?

8. After reading the various articles on assessment, how would you define "assessment literacy"? What do you think are the essential components of assessment literacy? In a journal, write down what you perceive as your strengths and weaknesses related to assessment literacy and steps you could take to enhance your knowledge and skills in this area. Follow up by checking off those steps as you take them.

9. Many people who are not early childhood educators do not understand how you can "test" a young child. They also may not understand the difference between casually watching a child and making systematic observations. Either in writing or in conversation, practice explaining differences between assessments of young children and assessments or tests for older children, and differences in casual versus systematic assessment.

10. In addition to assessing children in child development programs and schools, you can assess children in other settings—on playgrounds, at the beach or park, at home, while waiting at a bus station or in a doctor's office. What new insights can you gain from observing children in different settings?

Focus on families and communities

11. Some families may have strong reactions to child assessment in either a negative way (being fearful or angry about the assessment of their child) or a positive way (wanting their child to be assessed more frequently). Using information you have gained from this book, how can you help families have a healthy appreciation for the benefits and limitations of assessment? See if you can communicate the appropriate role of assessment and its uses to a parent or other family member.

12. Several authors mention the importance of gathering information about children's interests and progress from family members. In addition to conversation and anecdotal information, how else might parents provide information about their child? Create a list of items families might share, including samples of children's art, photographs, video recordings, written observations, copies of children's letters to grandparents, and so on. Distribute the list to families and encourage them to share such items with you.

13. All families love to see photographs of their children. How can you use photographs or videos to give family members a better understanding of their child's learning? Try using visual documentation to demonstrate children's progress. For example, you might create displays that pair photos of children's participation in an activity at two different points during the year, showing their improved skill levels over time. For families whose schedules don't permit them to come to the school or center, consider printing the photos in a newsletter, sharing them by e-mail, or putting together a simple photo album.

14. The NAEYC and NAECS/SDE joint position statement recommends that assessment of young children be "culturally and linguistically responsive." What does this mean to you? How might you translate that recommendation into specific actions you take in assessing young children? Why is it so important? Consider whether your current assessments acknowledge differences in family structure, ethnicity, socioeconomic status, religion, and so on. Examine the language, photos, or pictures in your assessments to determine whether they represent nonstereotypical depictions of various groups.

Identify resources and plan next steps

15. The **"Resources"** section (pp. 58–59) contains a rich menu of assessment-related books, articles, and Web sites. In addition, most articles have a list of references specific to their topic. Select one or more of these resources, and write an annotated description of it to guide others—perhaps putting the information in handouts or on a Web page. What is the early childhood content of the material? For which professionals is it especially valuable? For which children?

16. Besides those listed in this book, what other resources have you found to support your understanding of assessment of young children? Again, you might create an annotated list to share.

17. What areas could you focus on to better support appropriate and effective assessment of young children? For instance, do you know about and use a variety of types of assessment? Are you comfortable discussing concerns with families? Do you understand the different purposes of assessments, from informing teaching practices to gauging program accountability?

18. Develop specific plans to expand, enhance, or improve upon your use of appropriate and effective assessment. Create an action plan to guide this work. Implement your plans and record what happens through observation notes, journal entries, videos, or photos.